WRITERS AND THEIR WORK

General Edit
ISOBEL ARMSTI

Advisory Ed
BRYAN LOUG

11·1797
15
AAT- 1939

D0283530

Andrew Marvell

ANDREW MARVELL

From the NETTLETON *portrait c. 1655-60 by
courtesy of the Trustees of the National Portrait Gallery*

Andrew Marvell

Annabel Patterson

Northcote House
in association with
The British Council

© Copyright 1994 by Annabel Patterson

First published in 1994 by Northcote House Publishers Ltd, Plymbridge House, Estover Road, Plymouth PL6 7PZ, United Kingdom. Tel: Plymouth (0752) 735251. Fax: (0752) 695699. Telex: 45635.

British Library Cataloguing-in-Publication Data
A catalogue record for this book is available from the British Library

ISBN 0 7463 0715 2

Typeset by PDQ Typesetting, Stoke-on-Trent
Printed and bound in the United Kingdom by BPC Wheatons Ltd, Exeter

Contents

Biographical Outline   vii

Abbreviations and References   ix

Introduction   1

1   The Biographical Record   12

2   Religion and Pleasure   22

3   Hindsight and Foresight   34

4   Jest and Earnest   48

Epilogue   61

Notes   67

Select Bibliography   73

Index   79

TOC

Biographical Outline

1621	Andrew Marvell born at Winestead-in-Holderness, Yorkshire.
1624	The Marvell family moves to Hull.
1629–33	Marvell probably attends Hull Grammar School.
1633	Matriculates at Trinity College, Cambridge.
1638	Mother dies and father remarries.
1639	Receives BA; experiments with Roman Catholicism.
1641	Father drowned; Marvell leaves Cambridge for London.
1642–7	Travels in Holland, France, Italy and Spain.
1650	Writes *An Horatian Ode* and (perhaps) *Tom May's Death*.
1651–2	Tutor to Sir Thomas Fairfax's daughter Mary at Nunappleton House in Yorkshire.
1653	Writes *The Character of Holland*; recommended by Milton as Assistant Latin Secretary to the Council of State, but not appointed. Tutor to William Dutton, later a ward of Oliver Cromwell, in the house of John Oxenbridge in Eton.
1653–4	Writes *The First Anniversary*.
1656	Reported as being in France with his pupil, described as a 'notable English Italo-Machiavellian'.
1657	Appointed Latin Secretary to John Thurloe.
1658	Cromwell dies; Marvell writes *A Poem upon the Death of His late Highness the Lord Protector*.
1659	Elected Member of Parliament for Hull.
1660	Re-elected to 'Cavalier' parliament.
1662–3	Absent in Holland for unknown political mission.
1663–5	Accompanies Earl of Carlisle on embassy to Russia, Sweden and Denmark (as diplomatic secretary).
1667	Writes *Last Instructions to a Painter*; takes part in

	parliamentary impeachment of Clarendon.
1672–3	Publishes both parts of *Rehearsal Transpros'd* against Samuel Parker, archdeacon of Canterbury.
1674	Mentioned by government spies as a member of a 'Dutch Fifth Column' under a code name; writes *Upon Mr Milton's Paradise Lost*.
1676	Publishes *Mr. Smirke: Or the Divine in Mode*, under pseudonym of Andreas Rivetus, Jr.
1677	Lodges two bankrupt relatives in house in Great Russell Street; publishes *An Account of the Growth of Popery and Arbitrary Government* (anonymously).
1678	Publishes *Remarks upon a late Disingenuous Discourse* in defence of John Howe; in August dies of a 'tertian ague'.
1681	*Miscellaneous Poems* published by Mary Palmer, his housekeeper, alias 'Mary Marvell'.

Abbreviations and References

Unless otherwise stated, all citations of Marvell's poetry are from *Poems and Letters*, edited by H. M. Margoliouth, revised by Pierre Legouis, 2 volumes (Oxford, 1971).

PL1	*Poems and Letters*, vol. 1.
PL2	*Poems and Letters*, vol. 2.
Donno	Elizabeth Story Donno (ed.), *Andrew Marvell: The Critical Heritage* (London, 1978).
Kelliher	Hilton Kelliher, *Andrew Marvell Poet & Politician 1621–1678* (London, 1978).

Introduction

Society is all but rude,
To this delicious Solitude.

. . . . . .

No white nor red was ever seen
So am'rous as this lovely green.

. . . . . .

The Nectaren, and curious Peach,
Into my hands themselves do reach;

. . . . . .

Two Paradises 'twere in one
To live in Paradise alone.

IMAGES

These four couplets, culled from what is perhaps already the most elegantly *selective* poem we have inherited from early modern England, epitomize several of the qualities of mind for which Andrew Marvell is properly admired and remembered: precision, economy, control (over a considerable sensuality), a final eccentric solitariness. But someone who encounters for the first time the taut and teasing pleasures of Marvell's 'The Garden', and who wishes to hear more of this marvellous voice from the past, will have to survive several disappointments.

Among the earliest of those disappointments may be coming face to face with the heavy features painted perhaps by Sir Peter Lely and now in the National Portrait Gallery: big nose, pouchy cheeks and chin, mouth too full for a man, especially in the lower lip, the whole not so much redeemed as rendered problematic by the fine wide eyes and challenging gaze that characterize so many of Lely's portraits. On closer inspection, the 'Nettleton' portrait becomes enigmatic not only in its gaze but also in its iconography. The plain white collar or band, the plain brown jacket and skull cap share the

'puritan' semiotics of Lely's commonwealth style, most fully
expressed in his portraits of Oliver Cromwell or Peter Pett (whose
integrity Marvell would defend in his 'Last Instructions to a
Painter');[1] but the exuberant hair implies more courtly tendencies,
while peeking out from under the stiff band is some luxurious,
softer, shinier stuff, whose identification as tasselled bandstrings
does little to explain away the conflicting visual message. One
would have liked to know whether Marvell had fine hands to match
his eyes, but the oval frame (characteristic of Lely's portraits of
poets) excludes them from consideration.

Copied in reverse for the engraved portrait that appeared in
Marvell's *Miscellaneous Poems*, posthumously published in 1681, the
face is still heavier, the hair longer and more wig-like, the plain
jerkin now swathed in a cloak, the eyes warier over deep bags, the
mouth sensuous no longer. If one had to identify the expression, it
is Disappointment personified; or, as Thomas Hollis, the eight-
eenth-century republican connoisseur, remarked on yet another
portrait, the inferior one now identified by his own name, 'If
Marvell's picture does not look so lively and witty as you might
expect, it is from the chagrin and awe he had of the Restoration then
just effected. Marvell's picture was painted when he was forty-one;
that is, in the year 1661 ... in all the sobriety and decency of *the then
departed Commonwealth* [italics added].'[2] Hollis's interpretive bias
was perhaps not too far from the truth. If we allow the three
portraits, the 'Nettleton' (1650s), the 'Hollis' (*c.* 1661), and the
posthumous reworking of 'Nettleton', to represent the life, a
narrative of Marvell's gaze over the Revolution and the Restoration,
the story, like the face, succumbs to the pull of gravity. Whatever
self-contradictions were residual in the 'Nettleton' portrait (and we
can perhaps imagine the 'Nectaren, and curious Peach' had once or
twice reached themselves into those invisible hands), those who
presented his image to a reading public in 1681 wished him to be
admired for dourer, more reliable features.

The second disappointment that the curious new reader may
encounter is that there is no consensus as to what Marvell was
'really' like or for what achievements we, three centuries later,
should value him. In 1928 Pierre Legouis, Marvell's first modern
biographer, felt able to hold together (by more than alliteration) the
aspects of his career most likely to be thought an odd combination:
André Marvell, poète, puritain, patriote.[3] But in 1978, in one of the

several books that appeared during the tercentenary of Marvell's death, I myself noted that the critical tradition had by then enshrined a set of conflicting images: 'incorruptible patriot, garden-loving poet, metaphysical wit, Neoplatonic savant, the man of Puritan conscience, the reasonable loyalist politician, the literary critic disguised as a lyric poet'.[4] Had I placed them then in chronological sequence these alternatives would have been recognized as the product of historical shifts in literary criticism more generally; but in 1978 those shifts were less clearly visible than they are today.

The oldest and longest-lasting image of Marvell was part of the creation of a Whig 'canon' by such early liberals as Nahum Tate, John Toland, William Popple (Marvell's beloved nephew), Daniel Defoe, and the editors of successive volumes of *Poems on Affairs of State*. To this movement belonged Thomas 'Hesiod' Cooke's two-volume edition of Marvell's poetry in 1772, whose preface declared: 'My design in this is to draw a pattern for all freeborn Englishmen in the life of a worthy patriot, whose every action has truly merited to him, with Aristides, the surname of "the Just"'. This tradition is still reflected in Wordsworth's early sonnet, written about 1802, on the 'Great Men' that England, in contrast to France, had produced: 'The later Sydney, Marvel, Harrington, | Young Vane, and others who call'd Milton Friend'.[5] (See *Andrew Marvell: The Critical Heritage*, ed. E. S. Donno, pp. 6, 24). But as Wordsworth would change his commitments, so would literary criticism, which became increasingly uncomfortable with the idea that value in the writings of the past could be attributed on the basis of something so evidently disputable as a political ideology. The desire to write about Marvell *as a poet* rather than a political figure was visible throughout the nineteenth century and prominent in the first two decades of the twentieth; and although T. S. Eliot has been given the credit for placing Marvell in the foreground of his new poetics, he was apparently engaged in 'the plagiarism of received ideas'. (Donno, p. 18).

Eliot's essay was written originally for the *Times Literary Supplement* in 1921, to celebrate the tercentenary of Marvell's birth. It had two major objectives. One was to claim that the special frisson of Marvell's style, which for want of a better word we call 'wit', was to be found in only a very few of Marvell's poems, and was not peculiar to him, but rather 'a quality of a civilization, of a traditional habit of life'; the other, a corollorary of the first, was that this quality insulated Marvell somewhat from both puritanism and the politics it gave rise to, and hence *distinguished* him from Milton.

> Wit is not a quality that we are accustomed to associate with 'Puritan' literature ... But ... the sense in which a man like Marvell is a 'Puritan' is restricted. The persons who opposed Charles I and the persons who supported the Commonwealth were not all of the flock of Zeal-of-the land-Busy ... Many of them were gentlemen of the time who merely believed, with considerable show of reason, that government by a Parliament of gentlemen was better than government by a Stuart ... Being men of education and culture, even of travel, some of them were exposed to that spirit of the age which was coming to be the French spirit of the age. This spirit, curiously enough, was quite opposed to the tendencies latent or the forces active in Puritanism; the contest does great damage to the poetry of Milton; Marvell, an active servant of the public, but a lukewarm partisan, and a poet on a smaller scale, is far less injured by it. (Donno, p. 364)

Although there is, as we shall see, something in Eliot's sense of Marvell that helps to explain the contrasts between his different kinds of poetry, we ought to be suspicious of an impulse that not only privileges 'gentlemen' but selects as 'the really valuable part' of Marvell's canon only the poetry, and of that poetry only 'a very few poems'. We would now name this move hypercanonization. In 1966 J. B. Leishman's *The Art of Marvell's Poetry* carried to perfection the mandate given by Eliot and H. J. Grierson forty years earlier, situating Marvell in a 'metaphysical' mode (to be found in individual poems, or even in individual lines and images) in which he could only be distinguished from Carew, Crashaw, Cowley, Cleveland, and above all Donne by the finest of sensibilities.

Since the 1960s, however, as New Criticism gradually lost its dominant position, a rather marked split developed. Some readers rediscovered the Marvell of the Whig tradition, while others moved him into a world of theoretical play and meta-literary (as distinct from Metaphysical) sophistication. With the wisdom of hindsight, we can now see that the Vietnam War may have had something to do with this trend in North American criticism. Making this choice in 1970 were Donald Friedman and Rosalie Colie. Taking the other path was John M. Wallace (significantly a historian), who dealt almost exclusively with Marvell's political poems, satires and polemical prose. The politics/literature dialectic thus represented established the terms of everything that followed in the next two decades. The increasing presence of historians (and even political scientists) in the remaking of Marvell's political reputation was telling. On the side of 'literature as such' the claims had clearly been modified by a more inclusive approach than Eliot's. Thus in 1973 Isabel Rivers reformulated a three-phase theory of Marvell's career: intellectual exploration and play, followed by a strenuous relation between life and art, followed, regrettably, she felt, by the need to use literature as a weapon.

But it is not only the seismic activity taking place in academic culture and the real world outside it that can explain the multiple Marvells today's reader inherits. Though the same forces have competed for the spirit of Milton, Milton himself saw to it, by a mixture of intentional and unintentional self-description, that a powerfully unified personality was passed down to us as presiding over his own two-sided career. In contrast, Marvell seems to have been obsessively self-protective. His reticence was such that, when he speaks of himself in the later pamphlets or letters, the topic is almost always his reticence! In a letter of 1675, he rebukes Mayor Shires of Hull for having broken his confidence with respect to a previous letter: 'yet seeing it is possible that in writing to assured friends a man may give his pen some liberty and the times are something criticall *beside that I am naturally and by my Age inclined to keep my thoughts private*, I desire that what I write down to you may not easily or unnecessarily returne to a third hand at London'.[6] In another letter, to a friend in Persia, he advised, 'Stand upon your Guard; for in this world a good Cause signifys little, unless it be as well defended' (*PL2*, p. 324). In a 'Historical Essay [on] General Councils' that Marvell appended to *Mr. Smirke: Or, The Divine in Mode* (1676) he noted that the soul 'is only safe when under God's custody, in its own cabinet' (p. 127). And in the second part of *The Rehearsal Transpros'd* he declared that publication of one's opinions or beliefs is 'an envious and dangerous imployment':

> not to Write at all is much the safer course of life ... For indeed whosoever he be that comes in Print whereas he might have sate at home in quiet, does either make a Treat, or send a Chalenge to all Readers; in which cases, the first, it concerns him to have no scarcity of Provisions, and in the other to be completely Arm'd: for if any thing be amiss on either part, men are subject to scorn the weakness of the Attaque, or laugh at the meanness of the Entertainment.[7]

The relative scarcity, and sometimes the mockery, of the unmediated first person or authorial self in Marvell's canon is quite striking, not only in comparison to Milton's self-representation but also when one considers the practice of other seventeenth-century writers: Donne, Herbert, Jonson, Crashaw, Katherine Philips, Sir Thomas Browne, Lovelace, Herrick. Eventually, Marvell's habit of self-protection had become so ingrained that in his last surviving personal letter to his nephew William Popple, describing the reception of his *Account of the Growth of Popery and Arbitrary Government*, he speaks of himself in the third person:

> There have been great Rewards offered in private, and considerable in the Gazette, to any who could inform of the Author or Printer, but not yet discovered. Three or four printed Books since have described, as near as it was proper to go, the Man being a Member of Parliament, Mr. Marvell to have been the Author; but if he had, surely he should not have escaped being questioned in Parliament, or some other Place. (*PL2*, p. 357)

If this is not 'delicious Solitude', it is certainly a delicious irony, not fully explained by the fact that the *Account*'s authorship was, for safety's sake, supposed to remain a mystery.

No doubt some would say that the notion of authorial reticence is now obsolete, the mirror-image of a reified, bourgeois individualism or a pre-Freudian theory of identity. For all his reticence, Marvell discourages such thinking, not least by his scrupulous inquiry into what responsibilities authors incur when they intervene in the discursive formations of their time. In his *Remarks upon a late Disingenuous Discourse* (1678), written to defend John Howe against Thomas Danson, Marvell protests Danson's disingenuity, that is, lack of candour, in publishing his *De Causa Dei* only under his initials. *Anonymity*, not authorship, is a fiction, and in serious disputes an undesirable one; Marvell, who himself published his *Remarks* as 'by a Protestant' adopts this fiction while noting its cowardice. He offers to interpret the initials T. D. as referring merely to *The Discourse*, '*wishing that there were some way of finding it guilty; without reflecting upon the Author*; which I shall accordingly indeavour, that I may both preserve his, whatsoever, former reputation, and leave him a door open to ingenuity for the future' (p. 174; italics added). Yet the italicized phrase actually denies that texts can absorb responsibility (legal, ethical, political or in the eyes of God) for what their authors have said.

TEXTS

Today's reader ought to be aware that the difficulties of discovering the 'real' Marvell are compounded by certain editorial decisions, which have tended to obscure or shape the canon almost subliminally. The only edition that *may* bear some signs of his own intentions with respect to arrangement is the *Miscellaneous Poems* of 1681. It certainly shows the traces of political censorship or self-censorship. Marvell died in August 1678, and the volume was published under the auspices of a woman who claimed to be his wife, but whom almost everyone agrees was merely his house-keeper.[8] She also claimed that 'all these Poems, as also the other things in the Book contained,' were printed 'according to the exact Copies of my late dear Husband, under his own Hand-Writing, being found since his Death among his other Papers'. We have no way of knowing whether the poems, which appear to fall into certain logical clusters, were arranged by Marvell himself or by friends and associates; or what were the 'other things' they might have planned to include, since with the exception of a letter of consolation to Sir John Trott and two prose epitaphs, nothing *except* poems appeared in the edition. We do know that someone originally intended to include the three poems on Oliver Cromwell, 'An Horatian Ode upon Cromwel's Return from Ireland', 'The First Anniversary of the Government under His Highness the Lord Protector', and 'A Poem upon the Death of His late Highness the Lord Protector', since although almost all copies of the 1681 volume do *not* contain these texts, two surviving copies do. The decision to cancel these poems was probably made while the volume was actually in press, because even in the untruncated copies the second half of the elegy for Cromwell (lines 185–324) was missing, and may never have been set, thereby indicating with some precision the point at which the publisher lost his nerve or was otherwise inhibited.[9]

Why would the printer, Robert Boulter, or those who supplied him with Marvell's 'exact Copies', have been unwilling to risk recycling 'The First Anniversary', already published in 1655 by Thomas Newcomb, or presenting for the first time the 'Horatian Ode' and the elegy?[10] The obvious answer resides in the date of the *Miscellaneous Poems*, advertised for sale in January 1681, at the height of the Exclusion crisis, when the Whigs in parliament, led by

Shaftesbury, attempted to exclude James, duke of York, the king's brother, from the legal succession to the throne, on the grounds of his now-professed Catholicism. One early purchaser, Narcissus Luttrell, dated his acquisition of the *Miscellaneous Poems* 18 January, the very day that Charles II shut down the Whig campaign by dissolving the parliament. It was likely, therefore, that Marvell's friends decided that the message from the grave of a 'Late Member of the Honourable House of Commons' might succeed better if not encumbered by three poems unmistakably nostalgic for the Protectorate. Robert Boulter was actually arrested in July of that year, not for his work on the volume, but for seditious talk, saying that 'he did not question to see the monarchy reduced into a commonwealth and very speedily' (*PL1*, p. 241).

In the original plan of the *Miscellaneous Poems*, which survived these deletions, the most dangerous material was to have been placed at the back of the volume, whereas up in front was a disarming group of eight religious lyrics. The volume proceeds from 'cavalier' or metaphysical lyrics to a 'puritan' phase, marked by a series of epitaphs for members of Puritan families and three poems to or about Sir Thomas Fairfax, the parliamentary general to whose daughter Marvell had acted as tutor in the early 1650s; and the last section was completely dominated by the celebration of English republicanism or tributes to Cromwell as patriarch and international leader.[11] The principle of arrangement was therefore both prudential and thematic or ideological, rather than chronological; an important point that modern editions have more or less completely obscured.

Before turning to those editions, one other important point needs to be made about the *Miscellaneous Poems* as a source of information about Marvell's canon. One copy of the volume now exists in the Bodleian Library (as MS Eng. Poet. d. 49). It contains, on extra leaves added at the back, and mostly in a single flowing hand, the full text of the three deleted 'Cromwell' poems, along with a substantial collection of shorter Restoration satires. Of these, the 'Last Instructions to a Painter' had already been attributed to Marvell in a volume of *Poems on Affairs of State* (1689). Two other 'advice-to-a-painter' satires had originally been published under the name of Sir John Denham, although Anthony à Wood remarked (*Athenae Oxonienses*, 1691, vol. 2, p. 303) that 'yet they were then thought by many to have been written by Andrew Marvell, Esq.'. This 'manuscript' is now widely accepted as the one referred to by Edward Thompson,

Marvell's eighteenth-century editor. In his preface Thompson described how, when his three volumes were already complete, he 'was politely complimented by Mr. Matthias (Marvell's grand-nephew) with a manuscript volume of poems' belonging to Marvell's nephew William Popple, 'being a collection of his uncle Andrew Marvell's compositions [compiled] after his decease'. 'By this manuscript', Thompson added, 'I also find, that those two excellent satires, entitled *A Direction to a Painter concerning the Dutch War in 1667*, and published in the State Poems ... as Sir John Denham's are both of them compositions of Mr. Marvell; but as the work is already so largely swelled out, I shall beg leave to omit them'. He did, however, print five of the shorter satires in his preface, in the same order as they appear in the 'Popple' manuscript. With the exception of George de F. Lord and myself (and one interesting recent compromise) Marvell's modern editors and critics have either ignored this testimony, rejected it on the grounds of internal evidence, or been themselves constrained by a publisher's space restrictions to omit the 'Second' and 'Third Advice' from Marvell's canon. [12]

We must add, then, to our growing list of difficulties in comprehending Marvell the knotty question of what he actually wrote. And there are other problems of attribution raised by the 'Popple' manuscript. Did Marvell write 'Tom May's Death', 'On the Victory obtained by Blake over the Spaniards', and 'Thyrsis and Dorinda', poems that appeared in the *Miscellaneous Poems*, but are missing, apparently deliberately removed, from the 'Popple' copy?[13] One minor problem of attribution which does not derive from 'Popple', but has disproportionately affected the way in which Marvell's career has been conceived, is whether he wrote the 'Elegy upon the Death of my Lord Francis Villiers' attributed to him solely by George Clarke in the eighteenth century. Villiers was killed in a military skirmish in 1648, fighting on the side of Charles I. As Pierre Legouis remarked, 'If the poem is Marvell's, it is his one unequivocally royalist utterance' (*PL1*, p. 435). It would certainly add to the enigmatic character of the record if the man who wrote respectful poems to or about Fairfax and Cromwell had also written a royalist elegy in which Fame 'expects' to be able to 'tell':

> How heavy Cromwell gnasht the earth and fell
> Or how slow Death farre from the sight of day
> The long-deceived Fairfax bore away.

> (*PL1*, p. 429)

Given the frugality with words required of a British Council monograph, all problems of ascription (except with respect to the 'Second' and 'Third Advice to a Painter') will once more have to give way to space restrictions. But we must now return to the other editorial question – the arrangement of Marvell's poems.

Because of the excellence of its text and annotation, scholarly work on Marvell usually cites from *Poems and Letters*, edited by H. M. Margoliouth in 1927, reissued with a few minor changes in 1951, and revised and expanded by Pierre Legouis in 1971. Margoliouth selected a partly chronological, partly generic principle of order, which may have been unavoidable once the decision was made to abandon the *Miscellaneous Poems* as a *structure*, but was certainly somewhat arbitrary. The 'puritan' memorials were placed between the pre- and post-Restoration poems, with the exception of the prose letter to Sir John Trott, which was removed to the volume containing Marvell's constituency and personal letters. And, most strikingly, in Margoliouth's own words, 'satirical, commendatory, and political poems' were 'collected together' and 'arranged in chronological order' only within those categories (*PL*1, p. 225). Inevitably, arbitrariness is increased (to the point of guesswork) by the fact that the majority of Marvell's poems can only be dated hypothetically.

Margoliouth did not, even in 1951 when the 'Popple' manuscript had come to light, include either the 'Second' or 'Third Advice to a Painter'; a procedure rejected in 1968 by George de F. Lord, who argued that Marvell had written the 'Second' and 'Third Advice' and 'Last Instructions' as a series, a position with which I remain in agreement. Lord, however, came up with a completely new arrangement, designed to support his division of Marvell's literary career into three phases: lyric detachment, political commitment, and satirical disillusionment.[14] Subsequently Donno, the editor for Penguin, opted for 'chronological order in so far as this can be ascertained'; she also accepted as unproblematic the elegy for Villiers that Margoliouth had left in an appendix, refused to incorporate the 'Second' and 'Third Advice', and discarded several of the shorter Restoration satires that either Margoliouth or Lord had adopted.[15]

But editorial practice with respect to the poetry is only half of our difficulty. While Margoliouth's second volume contains an invaluable collection of Marvell's letters, and both parts of the witty and influential *The Rehearsal Transpros'd* were superbly edited by D. I. B. Smith for the Clarendon Press in 1971, there is as yet no complete modern edition of a collected *Works*. For the other tracts in support of toleration, not to mention the *Account of the Growth of Popery and Arbitrary Government*, on which was founded Marvell's reputation as a hero of the Whigs, one still has to depend on facsimiles, or on Alexander Grosart's *Complete Works*, originally published in 1875, and entirely innocent of annotation.

Without losing sight of the fascinating complexity that still makes Marvell compelling, I will try in the following chapters to reconstitute a complete (and not completely incoherent) image of the man, which will return him closer to the mixture envisaged by Legouis in his great biography. Chapter 1 will encapsulate what is known of Marvell's life and career, a story that contains some mysterious gaps. Chapter 2 will (bearing in mind Eliot's strictures against too narrow a definition of puritanism) examine the religious or 'devotional' lyrics. The third chapter will consider the 'Cromwell' poems as the place where he makes his allegiances clearest, but in apposition to the 'Fairfax' poems, as a site of the playful or 'pastoral' Marvell. Chapter 4 will offer some highlights from the Restoration satires and controversial prose; and in an epilogue I will return, finally, to the poems most often anthologized and taught, 'To his Coy Mistress' and 'The Nymph complaining for the death of her Faun'.

1

The Biographical Record

The two most important facts about Andrew Marvell, biographically speaking, are that (despite the misleading testimony of the *Miscellaneous Poems*) he never married, and that he spent almost two decades as a Member of Parliament for Hull, from 1659, when he was 38, until his death in the summer of 1678. Hull was his home town. His family had moved there in 1624 when Marvell was 3, his father, Andrew Sr, was a moderate puritan, appointed as lecturer in Hull's Holy Trinity Church, Marvell probably attended Hull grammar school, and his return to public service there (though he mostly lived in London) tells us a good deal about his way of coping with the collapse of the English republican experiment in 1659–60.

Between his Hull childhood and dutiful middle age, whose record can be seen in the nearly 300 letters Marvell wrote to the Hull Corporation about parliamentary dealings, lay not quite a quarter of a century of monumental events. Marvell's response to these, or direct involvement in them, has to be pieced together from a set of fragmentary records and hints, some of which are his own poems. First came nine years, starting at age 12, at Trinity College, Cambridge. Although he graduated BA in 1639, he apparently abandoned his MA degree shortly after his father's accidental drowning in 1641. Between 1642 and 1647 he travelled through Holland, France, Italy and Spain, in circumstances we do not know, but Milton later wrote to John Bradshaw, President of the Council of State (21 February 1653) that 'it was to very good purpose ... & the gaineing of those 4 languages'.[1] Hilton Kelliher guessed that Marvell left London soon after the outbreak of the First Civil War, and returned as soon as it ended.[2]

Milton's remarks were made in the context of recommending Marvell to be Assistant Latin Secretary to the new republic, but he was unsuccessful in getting his protégé appointed until 1657. In the meantime, Marvell was obviously making good connections on the parliamentary side. Early in 1651 he had entered the employ of Sir Thomas Fairfax as tutor to his daughter Mary, and spent the next two years at Nunappleton House, the estate in Yorkshire to which Fairfax retired after resigning his command of the parliamentary armies. And by July 1653 (having failed in his candidacy for the Latin secretariat) Marvell moved to Eton to become tutor to Cromwell's prospective son-in-law, William Dutton. Cromwell arranged for tutor and pupil to stay in an appropriately puritan household, that of John Oxenbridge, a new Fellow of Eton. Shortly after his arrival, Marvell wrote to Cromwell thanking him for having placed them 'in so godly a family as that of Mr Oxenbridge whose Doctrine and Example are like a Book and a Map' (*PL2*, p. 304). Oxenbridge's career included an escape to the New World (Bermuda) from the persecution of Nonconformists carried out in the 1630s under Archbishop Laud; and it is on the basis of this connection that Marvell's poem 'Bermudas', whose singers congratulate themselves for having escaped 'safe from the Storms, and Prelat's rage', has been, perhaps unwisely, assumed to have been written at this time.[3] The Dutton assignment seems to have continued through at least August 1656, when James Scudamore reported in a letter from Saumur in France that 'Many of the English are here but few of Noate such onely are The Lord Pagets sonne, [and] Mr Dutton calld by the french Le Genre du Protecteur whose Governour is one Mervill a notable English Italo-Machavillian' (Kelliher, p. 61).

Since leaving his own place of higher education, then, the only signs of Marvell's activities that have survived indicate that he had cosmopolitan instincts (enough to be thought over-sophisticated or machiavellian) and saw himself primarily as an intellectual, one whose relation to high politics would be peripheral. In the early 1650s the connections he sought, or that were sought for him, placed him firmly apart from the king's party, although, as at least his 1649 poem to Richard Lovelace demonstrates, he had friends among the cavaliers. It is often said that in 1650, the century's mid-point, Marvell was still capable of examining dispassionately the claims of both Charles and Cromwell to legitimacy and admiration. This view is based, of course, on the 'Horatian Ode upon Cromwel's Return from Ireland', which can be firmly dated by the fact that in May of that year Cromwell returned from suppressing the Irish rebels to take over the Scottish campaign. But to see this poem as the end of a phase (cavalier or detached) in Marvell's career begs a number of questions, and in so far as it rests on *interpreting* the 'Ode', the argument tends to become circular. It is true that its opening lines demand that 'the forward Youth ... must now forsake his Muses dear, I Nor in the Shadows sing I His Numbers languishing'. But it also seems to be true that Marvell intended this poem only for private circulation.

'The First Anniversary of the Government under His Highness the Lord Protector' was, indeed, written for publication. It was advertised in *Mercurius Politicus*, no. 240, for 11–18 January 1655, and a copy was purchased by George Thomason on 17 January. Yet Marvell's own place in the limelight, as this poem conceives it, is still in shadow. The shadow is Cromwell's. The poem was evidently conceived both as a statement of personal commitment to the Protector, and as an attempt to consolidate support for his regime, at a time when Cromwell was struggling with opponents of all kinds, from the parliament he himself had called, through the Fifth Monarchists and other extremists at home, to monarchist propaganda being marshalled internationally against the regicides. While Milton was tackling these forces in his Latin prose 'defences' of the commonwealth, Marvell was wondering aloud in verse whether Cromwell really was the apocalyptic leader he appeared to be, and cautiously imagining himself as a new prophet of the latter days, threatening with obsolescence the assembled monarchs of the world:

> Unhappy Princes, ignorantly bred,
> By Malice some, by Errour more misled;
> If gracious Heaven to my Life give length,
> Leisure to Time, and to my Weakness Strength,
> Then shall I once with graver Accents shake
> Your Regal sloth, and your long Slumbers wake ...

However conventional, the language of the Book of Revelations as Marvell applies it to the Protectorate has a sensible political interpretation: with good luck and good management, Cromwell will be able to consolidate the commonwealth on lines that are mutually beneficial to the revolution's leaders and followers:

> Hence oft I think, if in some happy Hour
> High Grace should meet in one with highest Pow'r,
> And then a seasonable People still
> Should bend to his, as he to Heavens will,
> What we might hope, what wonderful Effect
> From such a wish'd Conjuncture might reflect.

(*PL*1, p. 112)

14

But if that moment never comes, he will settle for the more modest role he currently holds, of the follower and observer from a distance:

> Till then my Muse shall hollow *far behind*
> Angelique Cromwell who out wings the wind;
> And in dark Nights, and in cold Dayes *alone*
> Pursues the Monster thorough every Throne.

(PL1, p. 111)

It is important to realize how 'hollow', to misapply Marvell's own word, this ambition quickly became. 'The First Anniversary' was written in the winter of 1654–5 when Marvell was still (presumably) a gentleman tutor. In September 1657, nearly four years later, he was finally appointed to the Latin secretaryship alongside Milton and under John Thurloe, Secretary of State; and almost exactly a year after that modest move into public life Oliver Cromwell died. As it quickly became apparent that Richard Cromwell was incapable of following in his father's footsteps an intense period of political infighting and factionalism began. It led inevitably to consensus that Charles II should be brought back to rule the country. Marvell's move, therefore, to official service of the revolution was belated to a degree that his own ironic perspective would fully have comprehended. Apart from the elegy he wrote for Cromwell at the end of 1658, which he had apparently planned to publish but which was withdrawn from the volume, Marvell's response to the cancellation of his utopian hopes was to stand for election to parliament. On 23 November 1658 he walked in Cromwell's funeral procession. In January 1659 he was elected to the House of Commons as joint member for Hull.

What sort of services did Marvell perform as Assistant Latin Secretary? He attended foreign ambassadors or envoys who arrived in England, as guide and translator. He produced, sometimes perhaps from dictation, letters of state and translated them into Latin. He translated from Latin a long political tract by the Swedish envoy in England, on 'The Justice of the Swedish Cause and the danger of the Protestant Cause involved therein' (Kelliher, p. 70), a project clearly related to the Protestant militarism of 'The First Anniversary', as well as to plans for a military alliance with Sweden that were in progress in March 1658. And from this point onwards, unsurprisingly, not only do the records of his career become more precise and less sporadic, but the signs of Marvell 'himself', that

complex of intention, conviction, self-knowledge and self-repre-
sentation, become less ambiguous.

Later, Marvell was to select not 1650 but 1657 as a turning point,
and not a very decisive one at that. In *The Rehearsal Transpros'd: The
Second Part* he wrote:

> for as to my self, I never had any, not the remotest relation to publick
> matters, nor correspondence with the persons then predominant, until
> the year 1657, when indeed I enter'd into an imployment, for which I
> was not altogether improper, and which I consider'd to be the most
> innocent and inoffensive toward his Majesties affairs of any in that
> usurped and irregular Government, to which all men were then
> exposed. And this I accordingly discharged without disobliging any
> one person, there having been opportunity and indeavours since his
> Majesties happy return to have discover'd had it been otherwise. (p. 203)

While there are several strategic disingenuities in this statement, not
least the redescription of Cromwell's protectorate as that 'usurped
and irregular Government', it is probably more accurate as an
account of Marvell's evolution than the neat division of his career
into three stages, lyric detachment, political activism, satirical
disillusionment.[4]

When Oliver Cromwell died, Marvell transferred his allegiance
unequivocally to Richard. A beautifully preserved autograph letter
in the British Library (Additional MS 22919) conveyed to George
Downing, the English diplomatic representative at the Hague, the
tensions in parliament following the death of the Protector. Written
at Thurloe's request, and dated 11 February 1659, it described the
difficulties facing the passage of a bill that Thurloe himself had
introduced for recognizing Richard as the new Protector:

> all hath been said against it which could be by Sr Arthur Haslerig, Sir
> Henry Vane, Mr Weaver, Mr Scott, Mr St Nicholas, Mr Reinolds, Sr
> Antony Ashly Cooper, Major Packer, Mr Henry Neville, the lord Lambert,
> and many more. Their Doctrine hath moved most upon their Maxime that
> all pow'r is in the people. That it is reverted into this house by the death of
> his Highnesse, that Mr Speaker is Protector in possession and it will not
> be his wisdome to part with it easily, that this house is all England. Yet
> they pretend that they are for a single person and this single person but
> without negative voice without militia not upon the petition and advice
> but by adoption and donation of this House ... But we know well enough
> what they mean ... They have much the odds in speaking *but it is to be
> hoped that our justice our affection and our number which is at least two thirds*

will weare them out at the long runne. (*PL2*, p. 307–8; italics added).

Marvell's 'affection' to the Cromwells was such as to render him sardonic when others who did not share it invoked the supremacy of parliamentary government over the claims of this new dynasty. He therefore differed strongly from Milton, who by February 1660, realizing that despite Richard's confirmation General Monck might succeed in reinstating both the House of Lords and the monarchy, had produced his own passionate argument *against* government by a single person.[5]

But for whatever reason, when Richard Cromwell fell from power in May 1659 and John Thurloe lost his position as Secretary of State to Thomas Scott, Marvell retained his bureaucratic position for six months. When the Rump Parliament was restored by Monck, Marvell forfeited his seat to one of the restored members; but in April 1660 he was re-elected as member for Hull to the new ('Convention') parliament that recalled Charles II. He was extremely active in committees in the Convention Parliament, being appointed to thirteen, including one dealing with the religious climate in the universities, for which he delivered the report to the House, and one appointed to recommend what was to be done about the army. As he informed his constituents in Hull on 4 December 1660, people were backing away from granting the king a standing army, 'men not being forward to confirme such perpetuall & exorbitant powrs'; and, he added, ' 'Tis better to trust his Mtyes moderation'. At the same time he reported to Hull, without a trace of 'affection', the dealings of this parliament with the leaders of the now-cancelled revolution:

To day our house was upon the Bill of Attaindor of those that have bin executed, those that are fled, & of Cromwell, Bradshaw Ireton & Pride. And tis orderd that the Carkasses & coffins of the foure last named shall be drawn, with wt expedition possible, upon an hurdle to Tyburn, there be hangd up for a while & then buryed under the gallows.

(*PL2*, p. 7)

These facts support what the earlier record could only make a matter of inference: that Marvell had an unusual capacity to conceal his private opinions. Having acquired credibility, he used it to good purpose. That same month Marvell spoke in the Commons in defence of another regicide, or at least the regicides' spokesman:

The famous Mr. Milton having now laid long in Custody of the Serjeant at Arms, was released by Order of the House. Soon after Mr. Andrew Marvel complained that the Serjeant had exacted £150. Fees of Mr. Milton.

Others seconded the protest against the punitive fee, and, despite the assertion of Sir Heneage Finch that 'Milton was Latin Secretary to Cromwell and deserved hanging', the Committee of Privileges modified the amount.[6]

But if Marvell approached his parliamentary career with the notion of saving what could be saved, he was soon to change his mind when the next 'Restoration' parliament took over. In the difficult months when the religious settlement was being negotiated, the bishops being restored to the Lords, and the Nonconforming ministers ejected from their pulpits, Marvell said nothing in the House, although he was later to comment bitterly on those events in the 'Third Advice to a Painter':

> The Lords House drains the Houses of the Lord,
> For Bishops voices silencing the Word.

(ll. 241–2)

On 8 May 1662, Marvell informed the Hull Trinity House of his decision to go abroad (on what seems to have been secret political business in Holland), and although recalled once by the fear of losing his seat, soon took the opportunity for a much longer absence as secretary to Charles Howard, earl of Carlisle, who had also been a supporter of Richard Cromwell, on an embassy to Russia, Sweden and Denmark, a project that lasted from July 1663 to January 1665. Cosmopolitanism, congenial political company, an interest in Sweden formed by his service to Cromwell,[7] distaste for the punishing temper of the Commons against Nonconformists, and dislike of the Act of Uniformity, all probably lay behind the various excuses he sent to Hull for abandoning its business for another year and a half.

It would be foolish not to see these journeys as another kind of turning point. By the time Marvell returned, Charles II was well embarked on plans for a war against Holland, supposedly a trade war, as Dryden represented it in *Annus Mirabilis* (1666), but suspected by Marvell as having a larger and darker agenda. It is probably not going too far to suggest that the 'Last Instructions', illegally published, would have been seen as giving not only an all too realistic account of the motives and misconduct of the war, but also literary aid and support to the enemy. For Marvell in 1667 the Dutch were no longer clearly 'the enemy', but a rather admirable opponent, whereas the real enemy were the various members of Charles's privy council. By 1674 Marvell was suspected of having joined a Dutch underground movement aimed at breaking the Anglo-French alliance and ending the *third* Dutch war, which Charles had begun in 1673.[8]

This aspect of Marvell's career would lead directly to the work that made him famous in his own day, the *Account of the Growth of Popery and Arbitrary Government*, published anonymously in 1677, ostensibly in Amsterdam, which drove Sir Roger L'Estrange into a frenzy trying to discover the author or printer. But between the Dutch war satires and that long pamphlet lay another stretch of increasingly disillusioned parliamentary service. On 15 February 1668, Marvell seems to have blown his cover as a moderate by speaking 'somewhat transportedly' of the incompetence of Arlington, Secretary of State, accusing him of having bought an office for which he had no capacity, and thereby endangering the whole fleet for want of proper intelligence.[9] Twice Marvell attacked a proposal favoured by the majority of the Commons to renew the Conventicle Act preventing Nonconformists from holding religious meetings. These speeches mark the beginning of his dissociation from his Opposition colleagues on the grounds of their persecuting temper. Over the next ten years, although he continued to do his share of committee work and report regularly to his constituents, Marvell made only two speeches which have been recorded. On 21 November 1670, he spoke briefly on behalf of James Hayes, under prosecution for attempting to subvert the Conventicle Act. It was not long before his silence in parliament became a matter of common knowledge.

If we want to understand Marvell's frame of mind in the 1670s, the best route is not through his later verse satires but rather through a text which, though not *intended* as a satire, became so by its candid record of his feelings. I refer to the long letter to William Popple, which serves as a kind of private journal of the House of Commons in 1669–70. 'You know', Marvell wrote:

> that we have voted the King, before Christmas, four hundred thousand pounds, and no more; and enquiring severely into ill Management, and

being ready to adjourn ourselves till February, his Majesty, fortified by some Undertakers of the meanest of our House, threw up all as Nothing, and prorogued us ... All that Interval there was great and numerous Caballing among the Courtiers. The King also all the while examined at Council the Report from the Commissioners of Accounts, where they were continually discountenanced, and treated rather as Offenders than Judges. In this Posture we met, and the King, being exceedingly necessitous for Money, spoke to us *Stylo minaci & imperatorio*; and told us the Inconveniences which would fall on the Nation by want of a Supply, should not ly at his Door ... When the Commissioners of Accounts came before us, sometimes we heard them *pro Formâ*, but all falls to Dirt. The terrible Bill against Conventicles is sent up to the Lords ... They are making mighty Alterations [in it] (which, as we sent up, is the Quintessence of arbitrary Malice,) ... the Fate of the Bill is uncertain, but must probably pass, being the Price of Money ... It is my Opinion that Lauderdale at one Ear talks to the King of Monmouth, and Buckingham at the other of a new Queen. It is also my Opinion that the King was never since his coming in, nay, all Things considered, no King since the Conquest, so absolutely Powerful at Home, as he is at present. Nor any Parliament, or Places, so certainly and constantly supplyed with Men of the same Temper. In such a Conjuncture, dear Will, what Probability is there of my doing any Thing to the Purpose? (*PL2*, pp. 314–15).

These outspoken expressions of frustration and contempt need to be remembered when one comes to Marvell's other famous prose pamphlet, *The Rehearsal Transpros'd* and its sequel. In these pamphlets, Marvell's response to the authorized return of religious intolerance in England was to conceal his hostility to the regime and to represent himself, as in the quotation featured above, a supporter of 'his Majesties happy return' and a promoter of the king's own policies. This strategy was enabled by Charles's Declaration of Indulgence of March 1672, which suspended all penal laws against both Roman Catholics and Nonconformists.

In both parts of *The Rehearsal*, Marvell selected a target who could safely be attacked, an ambitious young turncoat clergyman, Samuel Parker, who had abandoned his puritan and republican roots to speak for High Churchmen and the doctrine of required uniformity in worship. Marvell also selected a new persona, that of the 'Churche's jester', as he was later to define it in *Mr. Smirke*, or, as differently named by Parker himself, the Martin Marprelate of his day. The pamphlets, especially the second, were enormously successful; and the best part of the story is that Charles II was apparently willing to endorse Marvell's sanitized account of his own motives. The first instalment was printed clandestinely, anonymously, and with a saucy false provenance: 'London, Printed by A. B. for the Assigns of John Calvin and Theodore Beza, at the sign of the Kings Indulgence, on the South-side of the Lake Lemane'. After the first impression had been dispersed, Sir Roger L'Estrange tracked down the press and seized the entire second edition. Whereupon Nathaniel Ponder, a Nonconformist bookseller, informed Arthur Annesley, earl of Anglesey, himself a Dissenter, who summoned L'Estrange before him, and said:

> Look you, Mr. Lestrange, there is a Book come out (The Rehearsal Transposed [sic]), I presume you have seen it. I have spoken to his Majesty about it, and the King says he will not have it suppressed; for Parker has done him wrong, and this man has done him right, and I desired to speak with you to tell you this; and since the King will have the book to pass, pray give Mr. Pinder your licence to it...[10]

L'Estrange had to be content with a few minor corrections; and Samuel Parker went down in history as he who 'gave occasion to the wittiest books that have appeared in this age'. 'One may judge', wrote Bishop Gilbert Burnet, 'how pleasant these books were; for the last King, that was not a great reader of books, read them over and over again'.[11]

By the end of this brief study we will see that there was actually more than wit and jest involved, especially in the second instalment, and that the persona of the 'Churche's jester' is readily interchangeable with that of the 'Relator' in the *Account of the Growth of Popery*, for whose author L'Estrange was still searching when Marvell died, of a 'tertian ague' contracted on a visit to Hull. In a way, then, his story comes full circle: the circle being a figure in which Marvell was, as we shall see in the next chapter, philosophically interested.

2

Religion and Pleasure

One important biographical fact (or rumour) so far omitted from this story is that, as a Cambridge undergraduate, Marvell had a personal encounter with Roman Catholicism. Thomas Cooke related in his 1776 edition that soon after Marvell's arrival at Trinity College:

> his Studys were interrupted by this remarkable Accident. Some Jesuits, with whom he was then conversant, seeing in him a Genius beyond his Years, thought of Nothing less than gaining a Proselyte. And doubtless their Hopes extended farther. They knew, if that Point was once obtained, he might in Time be a great Instrument towards carrying on their Cause. They used all the Arguments they could to seduce him away, which at last they did. After some Months his Father found him in a Bookseller's Shop in London, and prevailed with him to return to the College.

And Cooke's anecdote was confirmed by the later discovery of a letter from the vicar of Welton to Marvell's father, reporting on a similar experience in his own family and asking for advice as to how to handle it. (Kelliher, p. 25)

This youthful truancy, which is how Andrew Senior evidently saw it, would not be of much interest were it not for the fact that, of the eight devotional poems that introduced Marvell's *Miscellaneous Poems* to the Restoration reader in 1681, three (or four, if one counts both the English and Latin versions of 'On a Drop of Dew') have Roman Catholic antecedents. Yet they share the privileged space of the volume's opening pages with 'Bermudas', whose imagined context is the flight of puritan settlers to the New World; and introducing all the devotional poems is 'A Dialogue between the Resolved Soul, and Created Pleasure', whose opening lines not only celebrate a plain style of religious experience, but might also be considered a symbolic retelling of Marvell's juvenile truancy: of Jesuit seduction countered by paternal, puritan restraint.

Courage my Soul, now learn to wield
The weight of thine immortal Shield.
Close on thy Head thy Helmet bright.
Ballance thy Sword against the Fight.
See where an Army, strong as fair,
With silken Banners spreads the air.
Now, if thou bee'st that thing Divine,
In this day's Combat let it shine:
And shew that Nature wants an Art
To conquer one resolved Heart.

(*PL*1, p. 9)

Taken together, however, the eight poems seem to argue that choosing one's religion is never so simple as the Resolved Soul's unidentified adviser believes. Their combined subject might be described as studies in the vexed relationship between religion and aesthetic pleasure, a problem to which they give incompatible answers.

While we have only a slender basis on which to assign approximate dates to most of Marvell's poetry, for the devotional poems we have no basis at all. They could belong equally to the period at Cambridge following his return from London, *c.* 1640; or to his stay at Nunappleton House, in 1651–3; or to the mid 1650s, when he was tutoring Dutton under Oxenbridge's eye; or to 1672, when he was thinking his way through the intricacies of law and conscience in relation to *The Rehearsal Transpros'd*; or individually to any of the above.

There is, therefore, no chronological reason *not* to begin with the clues to his own religious stance that Marvell provided in the second part of *The Rehearsal Transpros'd*. There he indicated that the depressing history of the European churches since the Reformation might lead, if not to relativism, at least to a moderate pragmatism:

The Magistrate only is authorized, qualified, and capable to make a just and effectual Reformation, and especially among the Ecclesiasticks. For in all experience as far as I can remember, they have never been forward to save the Prince that labour. If they had, there would have been no Wicliffe, no Husse, no Luther in History. Or at least, upon so notable an emergency as the last, the Church of Rome would then in the Council of Trent have thought of rectifying itself in good earnest, that it might have recover'd its ancient character: whereas it left the same divisions much wider, and the Christian People of the world to suffer, Protestants under Popish Governors, Popish under Protestants, rather than let go any point of interested Ambition. (p. 240)

23

Instead of castigating the Roman church for its irremediable decadence, as Milton did in his church-reform pamphlets of the 1640s, Marvell leaves open the conceptual possibility that it *could* have recovered the integrity of its 'ancient character'. More impartially still, he notes that its failure to do so by generating the great schisms of the Reformation has caused as much suffering to Catholics in Protestant states as vice versa. And turning to English legislation of the forms of religious worship, Marvell continued:

> Even the Church of Rome, which cannot be thought the most negligent of things that concern her interest, does not, that I know of, lay any great stress upon Rituals and Ceremonials, so men agree in Doctrine: nor do I remember that they have persecuted any upon that account, but left the several Churches in the Priviledge of their own fashion. (p. 241)

By contrast, the English seem obsessed with ceremonies or their suppression – though not, Marvell continued with a switch of tactics, of their own accord. Had not the 'Civil Magistrate', that is to say, the successive Tudor and Stuart monarchs, not been persuaded by the clergy to intervene in a matter 'so unnecessary, so trivial, and so pernicious to the publick quiet', the English wars of religion themselves might never have occurred:

> For had things been left in their own state of Indifferency, it is well known that the English Nation is generally neither so void of Understanding, Civility, Obedience, or Devotion, but that they would long ago have voluntarily closed and faln naturally into those reverent manners of Worship which would sufficiently have exprest and suited with their Religion. (p. 242)

Situating himself between the Nonconformists and the High Churchmen, both of whom at this point he suggests are intransigent, though the former more justifiably so, Marvell identifies a new version of the *via media* in religion, an essentially English version. However, he carefully avoids describing just what those 'reverent manners of Worship' would be.

Yet only a few pages later, the middle position seems to have moved implicitly to the left – towards the Nonconformists. 'I must still desire you to remember', Marvell warned Parker, 'that by Conscience I understand Humane reason acting by the Rule of Scripture ... in order to [sic] obedience to God and Mans own Salvation' (p. 248). And perhaps even more clearly in echo of

Milton's church reform pamphlets, 'Christianity has obliged men to very hard duty, and ransacks their very thoughts, not being contented with an unblameableness as to the Law, nor with an external Righteousness: it aims all at that which is sincere and solid and having laid that weight upon the Conscience, which will be found sufficient for any honest man to walk under, it hath not pressed and loaded men further with the burthen of Ritual and Ceremonial traditions and Impositions'. Again, a certain pragmatism accompanies the traditional Reformation language, and grounds it in experience: 'most Creatures know when they have their just load, nor can you make them go if you add more' (p. 246).

To return to the confessional vagaries of the devotional poems, I am no longer as confident as I was twenty years ago that Marvell's use of Hermann Hugo's *Pia Desideria* (1624) as the conceptual basis for his 'Dialogue between the Soul and Body', or of Henry Hawkins's *Partheneia Sacra* (1633) for the two meditations on a drop of dew, can be simply explained as appropriations of Jesuit symbolism to the service of a compromise religious aesthetic. These Catholic 'sources', one a Jesuit emblem book, the other a Jesuit meditative handbook, were discovered respectively by Kitty Scoular Datta and Rosalie Colie.[1] Along with the gorgeously emotional 'Eyes and Tears', one of dozens of tear poems generated by the Council of Trent's emphasis on penance,[2] they represent a style of religious imagination that is simultaneously self-punishing and self-delighting, half guilty consciousness, half exquisite sensibility. This peculiar mixture was a product of the Counter-Reformation, a systematic attempt by Roman Catholicism to reclaim as many as possible of those who had left the Mother Church in distaste for her fleshliness. The hypothesis was that, after half a century or more of iconoclasm, unmusicality, and the defeminization of religion, people were starved for the pleasures that only religion could offer in a presublimated form. It may or may not be significant that Marvell's flirtation with Roman Catholicism is supposed to have occurred in the year following his mother's death and his father's remarriage. At any rate, the poems that directly derive from Jesuit sources are not only posited on the tricky idea of sublimation, but also, as a result of the changes Marvell worked in his material, permit the poetic *experience* of sublimation (having our sensual cake at the verbal level, but reading it as spirit). Thus 'Eyes and Tears' offers the weeping Magdalen, 'whose liquid chains meet I To fetter her Redeemer's feet', as a model of the poet, but surpasses its poetic analogues (such as Crashaw's 'The Weeper') in the intelligence with which grief is transmuted into bliss. It is not only that 'Stars show lovely in the Night I But as they seem the Tears of Light'. It is not only that a single elegant couplet *explains* sublimation: 'The sparkling Glance that shoots Desire I Drenched in these Waves, does lose it[s] fire'. The unique Marvellian touch occurs at the moment when the poet encourages his eyes to indulge in their 'noblest use' by performing the gesture that shows us, for better and worse, what exclusively we are:

> For others too can see, or sleep;
> But only humane Eyes can weep.

> (PL1, pp. 15–17)

It is no coincidence, then, that the two versions of 'On a Drop of Dew' further develop this metaphor of the tear as an image, as nearly beyond the carnal as images can be, of the soul. In today's secular culture, we would restate this problem of imagining the soul as that of identity or selfhood. It happens that the twinned Latin and English versions of 'On a Drop of Dew' (which in Donno's and Lord's editions are separated, the former consigned to the back of the volume) are obsessed with a figure that today therapists use to explain the boundaries of the self and the difficulties of discovering or maintaining them: namely, the circle or sphere, here made more fragile still by being conceived as a drop of water liable to evaporation. Shakespeare (another early modern writer sometimes suspected of Catholicism) in *The Comedy of Errors* twice used a drop of water as a metaphor for an emerging selfhood confused by the demands of relation to another self – the psychological task of being either a spouse or a biological twin. When the Syracusan Antipholus describes his quest for his lost brother, he remarks:

> I to the world am like a drop of water
> That in the ocean seeks another drop,
> Who, falling there to find his fellow forth,
> Unseen, inquisitive, confounds himself.

> (1.2. 35–8)

And two scenes later, Adriana, wife to the Ephesian Antipholus, and believing she is speaking to him when in fact she is addressing his twin, reproaches her husband for his desire for separation, which she sees as a refusal of self-identity:

> How comes it now, my husband, O how comes it,
> That thou art then estranged from thyself?
> Thyself I call it, being strange to me,
> That, individable, incorporate,
> Am better than thy dear self's better part.
> Ah, do not tear thyself from me;
> For know, my love, as easy mayst thou fall
> A drop of water in the breaking gulf,
> And take unmingled back that drop again
> Without addition or diminishing,
> As take from me thyself, and not me too.

(2.2. 120–8)

For Marvell, who writes twinned poems, identical in their statement though in different languages, the idea of a precarious balance between self-definition and absorption is expressed also in the formal balance between the symbol (the dew drop) and its referent, the human soul:

> *See* how the Orient Dew,
> Shed from the Bosom of the Morn
>   Into the blowing Roses,
> Yet careless of its Mansion new;
> For the clear Region where 'twas born,
>   Round in its self incloses
>
>   .   .   .   .   .   .
>
> *So* the Soul, that Drop, that Ray
> Of the clear Fountain of Eternal Day,
> Could it within the humane flow'r be seen,
>
>   .   .   .   .   .   .
>
> Does, in its pure and circling thoughts, express,
> The greater Heaven in an Heaven less.

'See'. 'So'. Each sphere is a metaphor of the other. Neither drop of water nor soul can really decide whether earth or heaven, immanence or transcendence, contact or separation, inscribes its perfect circle best. The poem, then, by way of expanding on the mystery of the soul's embodiment in a corporeal system from which it cannot separate itself, admits the artifice of this formal arrangement, using a word, 'coy', that Marvell associated with both seduction and obstruction:[3]

> In how coy a Figure wound,
> Every way it turns away:
> So the World excluding round,
> Yet receiving in the Day,
> Dark beneath, but bright above,
> Here disdaining, there in Love.

At last the poem attempts to resolve the dilemma by shifting to still a third metaphor (added by Marvell to his Jesuit source), in which the Hebraic manna, fallen mysteriously from heaven to feed the chosen (but never described as spherical) breaks the symmetry. Two's company and indecision, three's intrusion and a partly desired violation:

> Such did the Manna's sacred Dew distil;
> White, and intire, though congeal'd and chill.
> Congeal'd on Earth: but does, dissolving, run
> Into the Glories of th'Almighty Sun.

(PL1, pp. 12–13)

The loss of a virgin selfhood, 'white and intire', but somehow inadequate ('congeal'd and chill') to the demands made upon it, is finally to be rendered orgiastic in the light of the Power and the Glory.

If one gives this poem the theoretical space it demands, and especially if one wonders why Marvell wrote it twice, once in the Roman language, the rumour of a youthful conversion to Roman Catholicism seems not only more compelling, but permits the thought that Marvell might never have completely abandoned the pleasures that Catholicism offered, even though politically he threw in his lot with those toward the other end of the ecclesiastical spectrum. 'On a Drop of Dew' has more affiliations with Alexander Pope's deeply erotic 'Eloisa to Abelard' (a male Roman Catholic poet's representation of a female conventual's unwilling sublimation of sexual desire) than it does with the stern religion and firmly delineated egos of Oliver Cromwell and John Milton.

Perhaps at the same time, perhaps not, Marvell wrote his brilliant adaptation of Hermann Hugo's emblem of the soul caged in the ribs of the body; but whereas Hugo's emblem merely expressed the desire of the spirit for release from the body, Marvell rewrote the conceit as a reciprocal experience of political imprisonment and torture by soul and body alike:

SOUL:

> O, who shall from this Dungeon, raise
> A Soul inslav'd so many wayes?
> With bolts of Bones, that fetter'd stands
> In Feet; and manacled in Hands.

BODY:

> O, who shall me deliver whole,
> From bonds of this Tyrannic Soul?
> Which, stretch'd upright, impales me so,
> That mine own Precipice I go ...

(*PL1*, pp. 21–2)

One could argue that if the soul's argument stands for a Counter-Reformation otherworldliness, the body's stands for the predicament of the young man dragged back from London to continue his studies in puritan Cambridge. Such a hypothesis may seem less fanciful if one compares this poem to Marvell's self-representation in 'Upon Appleton House', where towards the end the poet-tutor begins to take on the characteristics of the subtle nuns who used to inhabit the estate before Henry VIII's dissolution of the monasteries. 'Under this antick Cope I move', wrote Marvell (in the same neat octavo stanza with which he had marked the contested boundaries of Soul and Body), 'like some great Prelate of the Grove'; that is to say, like one of the High Churchmen, relics of the old religion, to whose disendowment the puritans of the 1580s and 1640s were committed. Deep in the woods of the Fairfax estate, the ivy licks him into reactionary beliefs and sensual relaxation just as, in 1518, the nuns' smooth tongues had seduced 'the blooming virgin' Isabella Thwaites into joining their exclusively feminine enclave; and other creeping and climbing undergrowths reconstitute, evidently to the victim's satisfaction, the prison and torture metaphors of the 'Dialogue between the Soul and Body':

> Bind me, ye Woodbines, in your 'twines.
> Curle me about ye gadding Vines,
> And O so close your Circles lace,
> That I may never leave this Place:
> But, lest your Fetters prove too weak,
> Ere I your silken Bondage break,
> Do you, O Brambles, chain me too,
> And, courteous Briars nail me through.

(*PL1*, p. 81)

Given this masochism, it is perhaps not surprising when 'Upon Appleton House' reveals that its Catholic/Protestant dialectic has been less than serious. The representative of puritanism is here, ironically, a teenage girl, his own pupil, Maria, 'nursed | Under the discipline severe' of the Fairfax family. At her appearance her tutor leaps guiltily back to an erect posture (like the Body 'stretch't upright') while the whole landscape straightens itself into a more decorous relationship with its governing figures.

Whenever, then, we imagine Marvell writing 'On a Drop of Dew' and the 'Dialogue between the Soul and Body', in the early 1650s he was still playing with the problem of religion's relation to pleasure, and assuming that the old religion was more addictive than the new. In 'Bermudas', in contrast, the poet speaks as a member of a holy community whose enemies are the prelates with whom the tutor had identified himself in the woods of the Fairfax estate. Yet these puritans are neither committed to 'discipline severe' nor opposed to natural delights. 'Bermudas' introduces a group of singers in an 'English boat', either on their way to or departing from a natural earthly paradise, and thanking their God for their preservation:

> What should we do but sing his Praise,
> That led us through the watry Maze,
> Unto an Isle so long unknown,
> And yet far kinder than our own?
> He lands us on a grassy Stage;
> Safe from the Storms, and Prelat's rage.

> (*PL*1, p. 18)

Their song is a medley of phrases taken from or reminiscent of the Psalms, particularly those devoted to praise and thanksgiving rather than penitence and self-flagellation:

> He gave us this eternal Spring,
> Which here enamells every thing;
> And sends the Fowl's to us in care,
> On daily Visits through the Air.
> He hangs in shades the Orange bright,
> Like golden Lamps in a green Night,
>
> . . . .
>
> He make the Figs our mouths to meet;
> And throws the Melons at our feet.

This vision of a natural bounty more generous than any real-life settlers were likely to experience resembles, though in the sphere of the religious imagination, the more polished and pagan earthly paradise that Marvell conjured up for himself in 'The Garden', where the fruits behaved with equal abandon. We can infer, therefore, that 'Bermudas' was a deliberate intervention in the ongoing debates among Nonconformists as to how much further reform was necessary. There were extremists who disapproved, for instance, of church music, set forms of prayer and any emphasis on the poetic as distinct from the doctrinal possibilities of the Scriptures. To encounter in this poem a group of New World settlers who create their own metrical psalm of thanksgiving (one infinitely more elegant than the 'Geneva jigs' of the Sternhold and Hopkins psalter) is to receive a reassurance that 'An holy and a chearful note' is not an oxymoron.

But 'Bermudas' also makes it clear that these singers will not be (have not been) distracted by the sensual pleasures of their earthly paradise from their missionary purpose:

> He cast (of which we rather boast)
> The Gospel's Pearl upon our Coast,
> And in these Rocks for us did frame
> A Temple, where to sound his Name.
> Oh let our Voice his Praise exalt,
> Till it arrive at Heavens Vault:
> When thence (perhaps) rebounding, may
> Eccho beyond the Mexique bay.

(*PL*1, pp. 18)

This aspect of the poem connects it to the crusading theme of Marvell's republican poems, to the long celebration of the 'Victory obtained by Blake over the Spaniards', with its New World/Old World context for the struggle between Catholic Spain and Cromwellian England; and to the fears of the foreign monarchs in 'The First Anniversary', fears that the republic's navy is stocked not with ordinary ships but 'rather Arks of War ... a Fleet of Worlds, of other Worlds in quest; I An hideous shoal of wood-Leviathans'. What 'Bermudas' expressed as biblical idyll and escape (including an escape from the 'huge Sea-Monsters') these Cromwellian poems recast as biblical epic and confrontation, with Reform Christianity imagined as the new imperial power.

But before we make the transition to Marvell's other imperatives, we should recognize a devotional poem that cannot be placed with confidence at *any* point on the line between the reformed and the unreformed religion. 'The Coronet' is theoretically (confessionally) indistinguishable, for example, from Donne's 'La Corona', with its explanation as to how a rather ornate poetry can constitute a 'crown of prayer and praise',[4] or from Herbert's 'A Wreath', a chain-link structure of repeated words, which ends with a prayer for directness.

'The Coronet' is a very different poem from 'Bermudas'. In place of respectable psalmic echoes, we are given highly ambiguous metaphors which may and probably do mean several things at once; and instead of the directed couplets which kept the Bermudan settlers and their audience moving forward to some goal, 'The Coronet' is woven out of a convoluted syntax which deliberately entangles the reader. Nevertheless, its argument can be followed. The poet begins by describing his conversion from secular poetry (tributes for shepherdesses), and the weaving of 'Garlands to redress that Wrong' from the very materials of the old abuse, namely the flowers of language. In the centre of the poem, however, there is discovered an involuntary flaw in this programme of reparation:

> Alas I find the Serpent old
> That twining in his speckled breast,
> About the flow'rs disguis'd does fold,
> With wreaths of Fame and Interest.

> (*PL*1, p. 14–15)

The poet therefore appeals to God to save him from his own complexity of motive, to destroy his 'curious frame' (both the wreath he has woven and the body that identifies him) in the mysterious hope that what is no longer worthy to crown his saviour's head will somehow crown the divine feet by being crushed underneath them.[5]

At the very end of his career, Marvell was still uncertain as to how far religious sincerity was compatible with art and intelligence. In the *Remarks upon a Late Disingenuous Discourse* (1678) in defence of John Howe, in which the question in dispute was partly being discussed in terms of the style of disputation, Marvell reminded his opponent that 'curiosity' had traditionally been 'taken in many several significations'. It could either be a 'commendable exquisiteness in things considerable and worth the labour' or an 'impertinent diligence' in insignificant or improper areas of inquiry, or, thirdly, 'a superfluous and laborious nicety; as a curious man differs from a diligent, or superstition from religion'.[6] To the end of his days, Marvell remained alert to the way one ideological position shades into another, and by the frequent slippage from good intentions to errors of commission. In the brutal era of identity politics – the secular equivalent of the wars of religion – we could learn a good deal from his unwillingness or incapacity to be locked into one spot on the spectrum of belief, opinion and commitment.

3

Hindsight and Foresight

Marvell's poems to and about Sir Thomas Fairfax and Oliver Cromwell belong together, since both men became famous for their leadership of the parliamentary army against the king's forces, though Fairfax withdrew from the limelight and Cromwell went on to become a world-famous state leader. In the 1681 *Miscellaneous Poems* the poems were to have appeared together in two related clusters, with three relating to Fairfax's estate at Nunappleton immediately preceding a much larger group concerning Cromwell, beginning with the 'Horatian Ode upon Cromwel's Return from Ireland', and ending with 'A Poem upon the Death of O.C.'[1] This arrangement represents both the facts of Marvell's life – his service to Fairfax preceded his service to Cromwell – and those of his subjects – Cromwell succeeded Fairfax as commander-in-chief after Fairfax declined to make war on the Scots. These signs of logic and intention have been only partially preserved in the best of the modern editions (Margoliouth's); and they were sabotaged by modern literary criticism, which early decided that, with the exception of the 'Ode', the 'Cromwell' and the 'Fairfax' poems belonged in separate camps.

By the standards of the school of Eliot and its successor, New Criticism, the 'Horatian Ode' was valued for qualities (formal poise and ironic distance) that actually separated it from its great historical subject; while the concept of a 'pastoral' Marvell created a strong temptation to turn the 'Fairfax' poems into statements of a world-excluding ethos, which then became magnets for other more obviously pastoral poems in the collection. But it might be more useful today to see the 'Cromwell' and 'Fairfax' poems as a series of studies, spread out over eight years, in a single problematic: is it possible to write with integrity about events that will later be seen, with the dubious wisdom of hindsight, as revolutionary, but which, from the perspective of an onlooker–participant at the time, are inevitably infected with bias? From the moment of Charles I's execution, Marvell was evidently alert to the historiographical imperative to accuracy and objectivity, and oppressed by the difficulty of its achievement. While he partly conceived this as a rhetorical problem (how to manage appropriate shades of praise and blame), he also posed it as an ontological issue of validity in historical interpretation.

Because the 'Horatian Ode' was unarguably the first of these studies, preceding Marvell's period as tutor to the Fairfax family, it is impossible to observe a strict chronology while keeping the 'Cromwell' and 'Fairfax' poems together in their original clusters. I shall therefore begin with the 'Cromwell' poems. The 'Ode', as its title explains, was written to celebrate Cromwell's return in May 1650 from fighting the rebellious Irish, whom indeed he had managed to suppress with notorious brutality. But it was also, evidently, written to explore the nation's traumatic turning point, its first experience of government without a king. Charles I was not the first of the English kings to be removed by his subjects for misuse of his powers, but he was the first to be publicly tried and executed. Marvell's opening portrait of this new political leader, then, could not have a single focus. The poem cannot be unmindful of that other head of state, the king himself, whose sanctified image (in *Eikon Basilike*) circulated in the royalist press as if to deny his headlessness.

At least in structural terms, it is easy to see how Marvell dealt with this haunting presence. He divided his ode into three sections. The first deals with the present moment, the difficulties of understanding such unprecedented events, and the demands they made on the principled observer; the second looks backwards to the recent past of the king's execution with a mixture of pity and admiration; while the third section looks to the future of a militant republic, though it leaves unsettled precisely what role Cromwell himself would play in its governance. All three sections (as the history of the 'Ode's' interpretation makes manifest) register the claims of competing powers and interests, and the asymmetrical strengths and weaknesses of the two men who had come to represent those powers and interests as if in a symbolic duel.

One of the most telling moments occurs when Marvell introduces a characteristic of Cromwell with which he certainly sympathized – a desire for privacy:

> And, *if we would speak true,*
> Much to the Man is due.

> Who, from his private Gardens, where
> He liv'd reserved and austere,
>
> .   .   .   .
>
> Could by industrious Valour climbe
> To ruine the great Work of Time.

(PL1, p. 92; italics added)

Marvell's point is that one cannot assess the cost/benefit ratio of a revolution without taking note of the personal price paid by those who advanced it. 'If we would speak true', we must remember that Cromwell may have lost as much as he seemed to have gained by his leap to eminence.

This theme of the difficulty of truthful assessment is not restricted to the 'Ode'. In the elegy that he wrote after the Protector's death in September 1658, Marvell imagined that it was still too soon for an accurate measurement of Cromwell's achievement. Death has brought him, like a great felled tree, down to our line of sight, but on a scale that is overwhelming from up close:

> The tree ere while foreshortned to our view,
> When fall'n shews taller yet than as it grew:
> So shall his praise to after times encrease,
> *When truth shall be allow'd*, and faction cease.

(PL1, p. 36; italics added)

This last line indicates that Cromwell's reputation may, in paradoxical relation to the dead tree, continue to grow, as the prejudices against him are attenuated. Towards the end of his own life Marvell was still pondering the problem of delay in historiographical adjudication. In one of this tolerationist pamphlets, he hoped that the Anglican clergy, whose attacks on the Nonconformists he was chastising, would 'have some reverence at least for *The Naked Truth* of History, which either in their own times will meet with them, or in the next age overtake them' (*Complete Works*, ed. Grosart, vol. 4, p. 156). For this defence of Bishop Herbert Croft's *Naked Truth*, Marvell for the first and only time wrote under a pseudonym, Andreas Rivetus, an anagram of *Res nuda veritas*.

This concern with truth-telling, which links the 'Ode' to Marvell's later life as a polemicist, should deter a reader today from drawing any hard lines between poetic sensibility and historical consciousness. But neither should we reduce the poems to the status of historical statements. The distinction between 'affectivist' and 'historicist' readings that developed around the 'Horatian Ode' is still worth making,[2] and has extension well beyond this poem, which has been such a lightning rod to different currents of energy in the academy. By 'affectivist' I mean, roughly, 'what the poem makes us feel'; by 'historicist' I mean, roughly, 'what difference it makes to the possible range of feeling that we *know* certain things about it', things that can not be derived from its text alone. Each of these crude definitions raises almost as many problems as it solves. The first is subject to the weakness of that rhetorical 'us', since readers of the 'Ode' have *not* always shared the same feelings about its rival protagonists; the second is subject to another version of the 'delay' syndrome which separates 'us' from Marvell; for whereas some of the 'facts' about the 'Ode' were obviously known to its author in 1650, others – what befell the new republic, the subsequent reputations of Charles and Cromwell, and still later the story of the civil war period in general, ('what in the next age will overtake them') – may secretly, in hindsight, affect our interpretation.

One might now, in a different sort of hindsight, locate the poise of the 'Horatian Ode' as somewhere between 'affection' and 'justice', the terms Marvell used to define his attitude to Richard Cromwell. His primary concern is, as I have said, with the evaluation of complex and seemingly unprecedented events. Yet part of his strategy is to find precedents for them that others will recognize. A series of unmistakable echoes from Thomas May's translation of Lucan's *Pharsalia*, that dark epic poem about the civil wars of Rome, suggests that Cromwell is another Julius Caesar, the destroyer of Pompey. Horace's 'Cleopatra' ode (1:37), which makes Augustus the hunter and the captured queen a noble suicide, was also somewhere in the genealogy of Marvell's 'Ode'.[3] One question these echoes raise is how far the analogy will hold. Will this new crosser of Rubicons himself be destroyed as a dangerous dictator? Or will he, as the poem's title alternatively suggests, become a wise Augustus to whom a new Horace (Marvell himself) may respectfully offer advice and warning? And how do these two late phases of Roman history, so often invoked during the English revolutionary period as analytic models, negotiate with the much older story recorded in Pliny's *Natural History* (Bk 28, no. 2, 6.4) of how, when the ancient Roman Capitol was being constructed, the discovery of a human head in the overturned soil alarmed the builders yet was *read* as a portent of good? Can the very different sight of Charles's bleeding head, whose owner had just died with courage and dignity on the 'Tragick Scaffold', really be dismissed by this learned sleight of hand? Marvell himself indicates that it cannot:

> *He* nothing common did or mean
> Upon that memorable Scene ...

In other words, the precedents for such events seem most remarkable for their refusal to satisfy, explain or predict. Does this mean that we should temper emotional response with the wary detachment of the historian who knows that all the news is not yet in? Perhaps. But perhaps it also means we should temper the historicist conviction that more knowledge can *explain* Marvell's attitude by the affective insight that major change both excites and terrifies. If one cannot have both the 'antient Rights' and the necessary revolution, the cultured, pacific, self-regarding monarch and the leader whom Marvell would, both here and in 'The First Anniversary', recognize as 'indefatigable' in the service of the opposite ideals, how do we choose? Indeed, *must* we choose?

Put in these terms, the question must also be answered by attention to the formal (poetic) qualities of the 'Ode', which Marvell certainly chose. Most striking, perhaps, is the rigid control Marvell exerts over his vocabulary, relying heavily on monosyllables, especially monosyllabic verb forms, not only to tell his story but to suggest its contested values and the demands it makes on the onlooker. By verbs of action and movement ('leave', 'cease', 'urg'd', 'went', 'rent', 'blast', 'climbe', 'cast', 'hold', 'break', 'wove', 'chase', 'clap', 'bow'd', 'fright', 'tam'd') he presents the inexorable force that Cromwell represents and its effects. By verbs of affective communication ('sing', 'blame', 'speak', 'plead', 'see', 'fear') he suggests the effects of 'greater Spirits' on weaker ones, including himself and the Scots. Against this stark primitivism, there stand out with startling difference his occasional Latinisms, where the values of the poems are condensed: Cromwell's 'industrious Valour', Nature's rejection of 'penetration' (two bodies occupying the same space), 'that memorable Scene' and, significantly repeated, 'that memorable Hour' at the scaffold. The charge to Cromwell in the last few lines to 'March indefatigably on' in the service of Protestant imperialism speaks volumes about Marvell's own value system, in which energy, decisiveness, and sheer hard work were what separated the men from the playboys. Perhaps most interesting, lexically speaking, is his ideological deployment of two seemingly weak indicators of action and constraint – 'did' and 'must' – which here are far from being mere semantic intensifiers or metrical space-keepers.

We have already seen that the 'Ode' begins with a charge to the literary or academic community to engage with more than words:

> The forward Youth that would appear
> *Must* now forsake his Muses dear,
>   Nor in the Shadows sing
>   His numbers languishing.
> 'Tis time to leave the Books in dust,
> And oyl th'unused Armours rust ...

(PL1, p. 91; italics added)

This charge, in which 'must' is both intensified by and contrasted with the rhyme-words 'dust' and 'rust', is to join the 'active Star' of Cromwell, who also 'could not cease I In the inglorious Arts of Peace', those precisely to which Charles I had been dedicated. 'Did' then becomes a sign of that militarism and its consequences. Cromwell 'did thorough his own Side I His fiery way divide'. Around the scaffold 'the armed Bands I Did clap their bloody hands'. The king's eye 'The Axes edge did try', the bleeding head 'Did fright the Architects', all locutions that express the facts of history, which are now a matter of record. Meanwhile, 'must' has been repeated at a more philosophical level, and implies that the replacement of the king is a natural process: 'Nature ... *must* make room I Where greater Spirits come' (*PL*1, p. 92; italics added). And 'must' reappears, significantly in distinction from 'did', in the poem's conclusion:

> The same Arts that *did* gain
> A Pow'r *must* it maintain.

(PL1, p. 94; italics added)

The irrevocable past and the inevitable future, hindsight and foresight, meet in a no-nonsense style that makes mere evenhand-edness effete, and that goes beyond ambivalence to a disciplined acclimatization.

At first sight 'The First Anniversary' gives the impression of loss of discipline. Some have associated its seeming incoherence with Marvell's transition from choice in progress (critical detachment) to choice complete (intellectual subservience and artless 'propaganda'). Conversely, others have moved to defend its 'unity', as New Critical protocols were invoked to defend one of New Criticism's outcasts. The poem is certainly much less crisp that the 'Ode'; and, while it invokes the straight-line trajectory of Christian history (leading from Adam and Noah, as founding figures, through Gideon and Elijah, as types respectively of upright antimonarchist and the inspired religious prophet, to Cromwell himself, imagined as the hero of the Apocalypse who will bring in the latter days), it does so in a far from straightforward or progressive way. 'The First Anniversary' is an exercise in readerly frustration. Perhaps this was precisely the intention. Perhaps the biblical types are intended to function in the same provocative but ultimately unsatisfying way as the echoes of Roman history inserted so unreassuringly into the 'Ode'.

What Marvell addressed in 'The First Anniversary' was, however, not exclusively a problem in historiography and ethics. It was also a problem of political *theory*, expressed as a shortage of terminology: how were the English now to define the unique position that Cromwell had achieved? What word, literally, would specify its powers and limits (if any)? Since the Protectorate was formally established a year earlier, through the 'Instrument of Government' to which the poem refers in an idealistic musical metaphor, Cromwell was recognized not merely as military commander 'still in the Republick's hand' but as virtually a dictator (very much like Julius Caesar). To some it seemed clear that since he held all the powers of a king, he might as well accept the crown also, and thereby settle the problem of who would succeed him in conventional dynastic terms. Some modern readers see 'The First Anniversary' as an appeal to Cromwell to do just that; and others have argued, conversely, that it casts the Protectorate, with its biblical model of the Old Testament judges behind it, as unequivocally superior to the monarchical model.[4] How can one poem produce two such different understandings? Partly because Marvell's most direct statement of this problem is lexically and syntactically ambiguous. Returning to the notion of Cromwell's sacrifice of his privacy to the demands of public life, Marvell released into his poem a series of paradoxes:

> For all delight of Life thou then didst lose,
> When to Command, thou didst thy self Depose;
> Resigning up thy Privacy so dear,
> To turn the headstrong Peoples Charioteer;
> For to be Cromwell was a greater thing,
> Then ought below, or yet above a King:
> Therefore thou rather didst thy Self depress,
> Yielding to Rule, because it made thee Less.

(ll. 221–8)

While a literal understanding of what is neither below or above kingship would seem to be kingship itself, this does not appear to be what Marvell means. Rather, the idea of what it is 'to be Cromwell' remains inscrutable, tilted slightly toward the idea of a selfhood for which all political titles are irrelevant.

Even more peculiar is the centre of Marvell's poem, where he dealt with the dangerous accident Cromwell suffered in 1654 when his runaway horses overturned his coach. Other writers, both sympathetic and hostile, quickly burst into print on this subject. The anonymous 'A Jolt on Michaelmas Day' suggested that Cromwell had only been saved for the hangman's cart; whereas George Wither's 'Vaticinium Causuale: A Rapture Occasioned By the late Miraculous Deliverance of His Highnesse the Lord Protector, From a Desperate Danger' left no doubt, from its unwieldy title onwards, of its support for the regime. Marvell's response was as different from either as it was characteristic of himself. He allows himself to become trapped in imaginative recall of the incident, and begins to describe Cromwell's death as if it had not been averted after all, as if the chariot had, like Elijah's, transported the Protector to heaven:

> But thee triumphant hence the firy Carr,
> And firy Steeds had born out of the Warr,
> From the low World, and thankless Men above,
> Unto the Kingdom blest of Peace and Love:
> We only mourn'd our selves, in thine Ascent,
> Whom thou hadst left beneath with Mantle rent.

(ll. 215–20)

The use of simple past tenses ('had born', 'mourn'd', 'left' and 'rent') promotes a feeling of loss and disaster; at least until Marvell reveals that this was just a strategy to promote his long-term project, truthful assessment:

41

Let this one Sorrow interweave among
The other Glories of our yearly Song.

. . . .

So with more Modesty we may be True,
And speak *as of the Dead* the Praises due.

(italics added)

From the perspective of fictive bereavement, the poet can achieve 'modesty' in his praise – a term that Marvell continuously used to denote an acceptable rhetorical stance, and that seems to combine sobriety of tone with an unselfserving agenda. Cromwell, we are asked to believe, arrived at his decisions by similar standards.

An important cluster of allusions by which Marvell sketches Cromwell's character derived from the Old Testament narrative of Gideon, one of the Hebrew judges who preceded the era of the kings. Gideon, a great warrior figure, also anticipated Cromwell in rejecting the offer of a crown.[5] After his death, the Shechemites crowned his illegitimate descendant Abimelech, who became a tyrant; a result prophesied by Gideon's son Jotham, in the famous fable of the trees:

> The trees went forth on a time to anoint a king over them; and they said unto the olive tree, Reign thou over us. But the olive tree said unto them, Should I leave my fatness, wherewith by me they honour God and man, and go to be promoted over the trees? (Judges 9:8–9)

The offer is repeated to the fig and the vine, who equally refuse it; but finally it is accepted by the bramble, a figure for the upstart Abimelech, who himself gives a sinister account of what his reign will be like:

> If in truth ye anoint me king over you, then come and put your trust in my shadow: and if not, let fire come out of the bramble, and devour the cedars of Lebanon.

After the deposition of Charles I, the virtues of Gideon and the wisdom of Jotham acquired a new relevance for Commonwealth theorists; but the irresistible connection between the trees' first choice of ruler, the olive, and the man who bore its name (Oliver) meant that the fable could be appropriated to Cromwellian supremacy.

It would be possible to argue from Marvell's language that he mystifies the political theory involved in accepting the Protectorate, creating myths in the place of precise and competing definitions. To some extent that is true; but if one knows the debates of the mid-century, one can recognize the following as distinct arguments. First comes (ll. 13–44) a devastating attack on *hereditary* monarchs, who 'only are against their subjects strong' because they rely on the concept of divinely instituted sovereignty to justify oppression, but have no other interest in religion. This is followed (ll. 69–70) by a brief jab at the 'tedious' theorists of the ancient constitution, such as Coke, Vane, or Spelman, who are still hacking away at their task of 'Framing a liberty that still went back' while Cromwell *produces* 'consent' by sheer force of will and charisma. Then comes (ll. 75–98) a subtle critique of Hobbes's concept of the social contract. Marvell argues both against some immemorial agreement of men to be governed in the interests of self-protection ('The Commonwealth then *first* together came' in 1649), and against the Hobbesian model of military dictator and subservient people, on the grounds that the self-interest from which Hobbes derived his system will not only continue into the contract but can be made a source of strength. The metaphor of architectural stresses and strains that Marvell employs supports, but does not conceal, his preference for a *more* egalitarian system than had previously been in place, and for democratic Parliamentary government:

> The crossest Spirits here do take their part,
> Fast'ning the Contignation which they thwart;
> And they, whose Nature leades them to divide,
> Uphold, this one, and that the other Side;
> But the most Equal still sustein the Height,
> And they as Pillars keep the Work upright;
> While the resistance of opposed Minds,
> The Fabrick as with Arches stronger binds,
> Which on the Basis of a Senate free,
> Knit by the Roofs Protecting weight agree.

Nevertheless, Marvell drew a clear line between his own concept of 'the most Equal' and the Levellers and other protest groups from the left wing who campaigned for a radical egalitarianism that Cromwell and the other grandees had never envisaged. To this end he reworked the biblical stories of Gideon and Jotham's fable to make them fit the second, sectarian stage of the revolution, and to make the case (which is both Hobbesian and anti-Hobbesian) that stable government was, in the last resort, more valuable than equality:

Thou with the same strength [as Gideon], and an Heart as plain,
Didst (like thine Olive) still refuse to Reign;
Though why should others all thy Labor spoil,
And Brambles be anointed with thine Oyl,
Whose climbing Flame, without a timely stop,
Had quickly Levell'd every Cedar's top.

(ll. 257–62)

'Tis not a Freedome, that where All command;
Nor Tyranny, where One does them withstand ...

(ll. 280–1)

While these lines indicate some of the challenges 'The First Anniversary' poses today – one needs to be fully in command of the original stories to which it alludes in order to grasp their often eccentric application – they are also completely in accord with its central message: one that, in effect, repeats that of the closing lines of the 'Ode'. Those who could accept in 1650 the need to 'maintain' as well as to bring about the revolution should now recognize that the need for maintenance was, if anything, greater, not least because accusations of tyranny might slide from the dead king to the indefatigable Protector. If the choice were now differently posed between the One and the Many, Marvell (and in this he was unlike Milton) had to choose the One.

This is not to say, however, that Marvell was completely confident of the rightness of Cromwell's policies, particularly given his refusal to work within a constitutional framework of government. Between 3 September 1654, when it came into session, and 22 January 1655, when Cromwell dissolved it, the Protectorate parliament fought to amend the terms of the Instrument of Government and to limit Cromwell's powers. And for all Marvell's rationale for the retention and exercise of those powers, he evidently imagined a better solution: that 'a seasonable People' could bend to Cromwell's agenda, 'as he to Heavens will':

What we might hope, what wonderful Effect
From such a wish'd Conjuncture might reflect.
Sure, the mysterious Work, where none withstand,
Would forthwith finish under such a Hand:
Fore-shortned Time its useless Course would stay,
And soon precipitate the latest Day.
But a thick Cloud about that Morning lyes,

> And intercepts the Beams of Mortal eyes,
> That 'tis the most which we determine can,
> If these the Times, then this *must* be the Man.

(ll. 131-4; italics added)

The ideal is political harmony, a 'wish'd Conjuncture' between leaders and followers. But the hypothetical syntax ('if', 'might', 'might', 'if') undoes the wishing and the hoping, and 'if' now qualifies 'must' as, in the 'Ode', 'must' was required to supplement 'did'. In the event, as Marvell's own elegy for Cromwell only four years later testified, those were not the 'Times' of an apocalyptic determinism or even a holding compromise. He was himself forced first to transfer his allegiance to Richard Cromwell, whose 'milder beams', presaged a different political climate, and then to observe, from within parliament, how neither justice, affection nor even number would be sufficient to hold back the Restoration.

THE 'FAIRFAX' POEMS

If the major 'Cromwell' poems seem occasionally to adopt a defensive tone about their subject's reputation, about the potentially dark side of his forceful character, this is another reason for reading them alongside the three poems in which Marvell attempted to describe the character of Sir Thomas Fairfax and to explain his premature retirement. That there was, in fact, a dialectical relationship between the two sets of poems is made clear by deliberate echo. Consider these interlocking couplets, the first from the 'Horatian Ode':

> So restless Cromwel could not cease
> In the inglorious Arts of Peace

and, from 'Upon Appleton House', the matching but contrasting description of Fairfax:

> Who, when retired here to Peace,
> His warlike Studies could not cease.

In this dialectic, 'inglorious' is never cancelled. And, despite the apparent symmetry, we learn that Fairfax's warlike studies at Nunappleton consisted in simulating battlefields in formal flower-beds.

45

Marvell approached this delicate issue obliquely. The three estate poems, 'Epigramma in Duos montes', 'Upon the Hill and Grove in Bill-borow', and 'Upon Appleton House' itself, all adopt the ruse of praising Fairfax's character symbolically, as reflected in some aspect of the landscape property he owned. The premise must be, of course, that retirement is not weakness (an embarrassing possibility made worse by the rumour that the strong influence of Lady Fairfax, who opposed the king's execution, was behind it), but rather a combination of strength with self-restraint. In both the 'Epigramma' and 'Upon the Hill and Grove' the conceit is worked out in terms of mountainous (and male) ambition versus a smoother (more feminine) mental landscape. The Latin poem was considerably less successful in this than its English counterpart because it represented Fairfax as a split personality, half Amos Cliff and half Bilborough Hill; whereas in the English version he is figured only in the nicely-rounded Bilborough Hill:

> See how the arched Earth does here
> Rise in a perfect Hemisphere!

This hill ascends courteously, and 'all the way it rises bends', whereas Cromwell appears as the most probable referent of the 'Mountains more unjust, | Which to abrupter greatness thrust', and for whose 'excrescence ill design'd | Nature must a new Center find'.

We should remember that when Marvell wrote these poems he had not yet thrown in his lot with Cromwell; it may even have been that this dialectical relationship between the 'Ode' and 'Upon the Hill and Grove' spoke to genuine indecision as to whether discretion was not the better part of valour in the early 1650s. Even so, 'Upon Appleton House' seems peculiarly wary of outright praise of Fairfax, who never appears in person, his place usurped by his firmly characterized daughter. While Marvell does suggest that Fairfax's motives for retirement were idealistic if mysterious – he mentions the 'prickling leaf' of Conscience, 'which shrinks at ev'ry touch' of human inspection – he precedes this justification with several stanzas that develop the idea of Fairfax's commitment to gardening into something remarkably close to a reproach. England itself is presented as a greater garden ('that dear and happy Isle | The Garden of the World ere while') that Fairfax has abandoned for Nunappleton, in a political version of the Fall. On the role of Eve in this lapsarian myth Marvell is, however, scrupulously silent.

The strategy of the poem seems to be to shift the burden of critique, if that is not too strong a term for this playful poem, to the over-imaginative tutor who is everywhere present as a figure as well as a speaker in this poem, and who weaves his way through the landscape, turning its scenes into myths, emblems, and philosophical conceits. After he leaves the gardens, with their 'five imaginary Forts' constructed by Fairfax, the tutor wanders through the hay-meadows, which he himself transforms into a 'Camp of Battail newly fought: I Where, as the Meads with Hay, the Plain I Lyes quilted ore with Bodies slain'. Real blood is shed when a meadow bird, the rail, is sliced by a mower's scythe. But these military metaphors have no more priority in the tutor's mind than other comparisons he makes – the smooth surface of the villagers' common fields compared to a canvas stretched for Lely to paint on, or for the Levellers to 'take Pattern at'. This easy going allusion to the problem that Marvell would tackle with evident anxiety in 'The First Anniversary' is a key both to the tone of this poem and to his own self-characterization, which eventually becomes explicit when he moves from the fields to the woods of the estate, and produces a meditation on trees very different from Jotham's fable or the image of Cromwell as 'the sacred oak' of the elegy. Here, in the woods of Nunappleton, the tutor becomes a disinterested spectator of how the 'hollow Oak' is mined by the woodpecker, whose role is to select which trees are 'fit to stand and which to fell' (l. 544). Is this a moral or a political allegory? This poem will never tell. Within its 'sober Frame' of neatly squared stanzas, the imagination has absolute rule, but its rule is benign. The 'Oake seems to fall content, I Viewing the Treason's Punishment' (ll. 559–60), and the poet indulges in a 'light Mosaic' of speculation, an intellectual medley of what 'Rome, Greece, Palestine, ere said', a little like elevator music. It is a telling final twist that when Marvell mentions the 'Discipline severe' of Fairfax and his wife, the reference is merely to their daughter's upbringing and their plans for her marriage, supposedly for some 'universal good': the irony that we may now feel in learning that they made 'their Destiny *their* Choice' in this matter may not be entirely the effect of hindsight.

47

4

Jest and Earnest

In the opening sections of the second part of *The Rehearsal Transpros'd*, Marvell articulated his doubts about satire as an instrument of political or religious engagement. 'For 'tis better', he wrote:

> that evil men be left in an undisturbed possession of their repute ... then that the Exchange and Credit of mankind should be universally shaken ... how can the Author of an Invective, though never so truely founded, expect approbation ... who, in a world all furnished with subjects of praise, instruction, and learned inquiry, shall studiously chuse and set himself apart to comment upon the blemishes and imperfections of some particular person? (p. 161)

Nevertheless, Marvell proceeded to write the second part in only a slightly less mocking and savage tone than the first. And in fact his justification for doing so followed immediately upon this expression of anxiety and principle:

> And yet nevertheless, and all that has been said before being granted, it may so chance that to write, and that Satyrically ... may be not only excusable but necessary. (p. 163)

In this case, the excuse is supplied by the fact that Parker's superiors in the ecclesiastical hierarchy have failed to curb his excesses, and the necessity by Marvell's belief that these excesses of tone and doctrine threaten the peace of the church. If Marvell had been asked to defend correspondingly his verse satires directed against the ministers and military officials of the Restoration government in the mid 1660s, he would surely have claimed that *their* excesses and failures of public responsibility threatened the welfare and safety of the state.

Unsurprisingly, Marvell was only half convinced by his own rationale; for he added, as a commentary on the first part of *The Rehearsal Transpros'd*, 'It hath been thus far the odiousest task that ever I undertook, and has look't to be all the while like the cruelty of a Living Dissection, which, however it may tend to publick instruction, and though I have pick'd out the most noxious

Creature to be anatomiz'd, yet doth scarse excuse or recompense the offensiveness of the scent and fouling of my fingers' (p. 185). This self-disgust implies that Marvell might have shared with some of his modern readers their view of his verse satires, which have most often been treated, if treated at all, with a mixture of wariness and distaste. Between the continued doubt as to which satires are indisputably Marvell's, and the suppressed wish that none of them were, few critics have paid much attention to them, with the 'Last Instructions to a Painter' being only a slight exception to this rule.

To repeat, I believe that Marvell wrote not only the 'Last Instructions', but also the 'Second' and 'Third Advice'. I base this conviction not only on the textual evidence of the Popple manuscript, but on the coherence – intellectual, political, and metaphorical – of the series of three poems. The whole series depends not only on the 'advice-to-a-painter' device deployed by Edmund Waller, and to which Marvell replied in kind, but on a more serious understanding of the use of the visual arts to define a political culture. Beginning in the reign of James I, under the patronage of figures like Arundel, Buckingham, Northampton, Carr, and rising to a peak under Charles I, the Stuart commitment to art collection is now well documented and understood; and royal or aristocratic commissions to continental artists for portraits, allegorical theme paintings and heroic landscapes made paintings an unavoidable context for the activities of the political nation. Also, any educated person would have been familiar with the names and styles of the major painters past or current: Michelangelo, Van Dyke, Lely, Rubens. Marvell's readers were equally at home with the classical formulas on aesthetics (Horace's *ut pictura poesis*, from which grew the *paragone* or rivalry between painting and poetry, or his famous provision, in the opening lines of the *Ars Poetica*, for a certain imaginative licence that breaks decorum: ' Pictoribus atque poetis I Quidlibet audendi semper fuit aequa potestas'); and they knew the anecdotes from Pliny's *Natural History* about ancient painters such as Apelles, Protogenes and Zeuxis, particularly since they encapsulated venerable problems of mimesis, such as the conflict between realism and idealism.

This conflict was central to the ways in which painting was appropriated and thematized by the Stuart courts, both before and after the revolutionary period, and statements about it were often expressions of political allegiance. In 1656 Abraham Cowley commemorated the death of Van Dyck, the most idealizing of Charles I's portraitists, in language that manifestly mourned the king as much as the painter:

> Vandike is Dead; but what Bold Muse shall dare
> (Though Poets in that word with Painters share)
> T'expresse her sadness. Poesie must become
> An Art, like Painting here, an Art that's Dumbe.[1]

Sir William Sanderson's *Graphice* (1658) actually featured a portrait of the deceased Charles I. Repeating the story of how Zeuxis of Croton created his portrait of Aphrodite by abstracting the best features from a number of less than perfect models, Sanderson advised the portrait painter to gather 'from several beauties ... a conceived Idea ... of accomplished Pulchritude, grace or comlinesse, according to the true rule of Symmetry' (p. 46). Presumably the king's portrait was an example of Symmetry's 'true rule' in more senses than one.

To understand Marvell's 'painter' poems, however, we need to place the ideology of Stuart pictorialism in a historical frame at once broader and more specific. The satires were written in response to the second Anglo-Dutch war on which Charles II had embarked in November 1664, ostensibly on the grounds that this too (like the previous war against the Dutch republic that Cromwell had ended in 1653) was required to settle commercial and colonial rivalry between the two nations. Perhaps now to his embarrassment, Marvell had written an anti-Dutch satire, ('The Character of Holland') in relation to the earlier conflict, a satire based on that cheapest of jokes, the caricature of national character; and still more awkwardly, his poem was republished, anonymously and presumably without his consent, in 1665; for by this time Marvell, who had already been on secret political business in Holland, was more sympathetic to the Dutch and contemptuous of the English in their conduct of the war. In October 1665 he had been appointed to a parliamentary committee to investigate one aspect of that conduct, the embezzlement of prize goods taken from the Dutch fleet,[2] and on 3 December 1666 he had written to Mayor Franke in Hull describing the efforts of the House of Commons to determine how the unprecedented funds voted to support the war, a total of three and a quarter million pounds, had disappeared without any tangible success to show for it.[3] As for tangible success, although the duke of York had won a significant victory at the Battle of Lowestoft in June 1665, on the same date the following year it was cancelled by an equally significant defeat, largely as a result of the imprudent division of naval command between Prince Rupert and General George Monck, who had earlier been a major agent of the Restoration.

Marvell might, however, never have intervened in these events in a non-parliamentary way had it not been for the provocation given by other poets. In the spring of 1666, Edmund Waller, who had once been Cromwell's panegyrist, published a long poem entitled *Instructions to a Painter, For the Drawing of the Posture and Progress of His Majesties Forces at Sea*, which presented the duke of York's victory as a symbol of the heroic conduct and high motives of the war in general. In it a device (derived ultimately from the *Greek Anthology*) of giving poetic advice to a portrait painter was transferred to the different art of epic or heroic seascape painting; and Waller argued the superiority of poetry over painting for drawing out the ideal aspects of the war: only words can truly 'Light and Honour to Brave Actions Yield, | Hid in the Smoak and Tumult of the Field' (p. 16). The following year, John Dryden (who had also begun his career by eulogizing Cromwell) followed Waller's example by writing his *Annus Mirabilis*, which attempted to alleviate public alarm over the two most disastrous events of 1666, the Four Days' Battle of June and the Great Fire of London in September. Marvell had been appointed to the parliamentary committee to investigate the causes of the fire;[4] but he would have been equally alerted to this issue by the appearance of Dryden's poem, calmly declaring 1666 'the most heroick Subject that any Poet could desire'.[5] Dryden praised the king's wisdom in dividing the fleet, interpreted General Monck's narrow escape, which had included having his breeches shot off, as 'naked Valour', and implied that the fire had been started by Nonconformists.

The 'Second Advice to a Painter', an unlicensed pamphlet, was clearly a response to Waller's poem, which it countered by substituting realism for idealism. The painter is asked to 'draw the Battle terribler to show | Than the Last Judgement was of Angelo' (l. 112),[6] that is, in the style of Michelangelo's *terribilitas*, often condemned as much as it was admired for its shocking veracity. But the real nature of battle, 'The noise, the smoke, the sweat, the fire, the blood, | Are not to be expressed nor understood' (ll. 207–8) by either painter or poet, but only by those who have actually experienced it. Moreover, the 'Advice' refuses to assume that all who fought were brave. 'Death picks the valiant out, the cow'rds survive' (l. 220). Most importantly, the 'Advice' provides a facetiously bemused summary of the motives for fighting the war, and its practical results:

> Thus having fought we know not why, as yet,
> We've done we know not what nor what we get:
> If to espouse the ocean all the pains,
> Princes unite and will forbid the banns;
>
> .   .   .   .
>
> Or if the House of Commons to repay,
> Their prize commissions are transferred away;
>
> .   .   .   .
>
> And with four millions vainly givn as spent,
> And with five millions more of detriment,
> Our sum amounts yet only to have won
> A bastard Orange for pimp Arlington.

(ll. 317 ff.)[7]

In other words, the fiscal concerns that we know Marvell to have been investigating as a Member of Parliament are here enumerated as proof that the war was, at the very least, a serious miscalculation.

There are not only similarities of interest. Those who have denied that Marvell could have written the 'Second Advice' have overlooked the remarkable similarity between these lines in the satire, spoken by a cynical sailor:

> Noah be damned and all his race accursed,
> That in sea brine did pickle timber first!
> *What though he planted vines*! He pines cut down-
> He taught us how to drink and how to drown.
> He first built ships and in that wooden wall,
> *Saving but eight*, e'er since endangers all ...

(ll. 135–40; italics added)

and these from 'The First Anniversary' comparing Cromwell to Noah:

> Thou, and thine House, *like Noahs Eight* did rest,
> Left by the Warrs Flood on the Mountains crest:
> And the large Vale lay subject to thy Will,
> Which thou but as an Husbandman wouldst Till:
> And only didst for others *plant the Vine*
> Of Liberty, not drunken with its Wine.

(ll. 283–8 ; italics added)

The two passages share the typological features of Noah as the inventor of both shipping and viniculture, the belief that civilization after the Flood was restarted with eight persons, and the application of these conventions to a modern wartime situation. They evince the same witty command over the old legend and its reappropriation, the same management of a few well-constructed pentameter couplets.

Finally, copying Waller's device of adding a concluding section of advice and compliment 'To the King', Marvell added counter-advice. Charles II is urged to exterminate the 'swarms of insects', who 'intercept our sun', that is, his venal advisers, especially the man here held most responsible for the war, Edward Hyde, earl of Clarendon. The king is urged to look upwards for his policy, to 'those kingdoms calm of joy and light | Where's universal triumph but no fight', and, in a nice *double entendre* (reminiscent of Marvell's wittier lyrics), to 'let Justice only draw', combining the operations of sword and pencil in an injunction to make peace with the Dutch and embark on reforms at home.

The 'Second Advice' was soon followed by a 'Third Advice' 'written by the same Hand as the former was'. In the published pamphlet which contained both satires, the title page carried a familiar, but also unfamiliar, Latin motto: 'Pictoribus atque Poetis, | Quidlibet Audendi semper fuit potestas. | Humano Capiti cervicem pictor equinam, | Jungere si velit.' That is, it *combined* Horace's claim that both painters and poets had always been allowed a certain amount of audacity with his seemingly conflicting statement that it would be ridiculous to place a human head on a horse's neck. Strung together out of context, the two classical statements now appeared to authorize poets and painters daring (*audendi*) to portray unnatural monsters.

The 'Third Advice' begins by rejecting Sir Peter Lely (perhaps Marvell's own portraitist) as the painter of the moment because of his potentially divided allegiance ('Lely's a Dutchman, danger in his art'). Instead it calls on Richard Gibson, who, as a miniaturist often copied Lely's work, to represent the actual (minimal) size of the English achievements. But the painter is also instructed to abandon the realism of the previous poem; a decorous concealment is now necessary to save the nation's honour:

> Ah, rather than transmit our scorn to fame,
> Draw curtains, gentle artist, o'er this shame.

(ll. 105-6)

In obvious parody of the draping to which Michelangelo's *Last Judgement* was subject, Gibson is asked to 'conceale, as honour would, his Grace's Bum', that is to say, the embarrassment of General Monck's wound in the buttock. But shortly afterwards this pose is suddenly dropped. Commenting upon the bonfires ordered in London to celebrate this 'empty Triumph', the poem introduces a new speaker, Monck's own wife, the duchess of Albermarle, who (as herself a Nonconformist) takes a dark view of the Restoration court. Revealing herself as also a prophetess (though one far less optimistic than was Marvell in 'The First Anniversary'), she warns that all these dire events are connected in history's deep structure, and that London will indeed become another Troy if the nation fails to understand the meaning of the year's catastrophes. The last section of direct advice 'To the king' warns him to hear this 'Cassandra's song', which in turn is related to the opening Horatian epigraphs:

> What servants will conceal and couns'lers spare
> To tell, the painter and the poet dare.

The 'Last Instructions to a Painter' declares in its title its intention to end a series. More to the point, it clearly indicates in its first line that the completed series will consist of three portraits of the nation:

> After two sittings, now our Lady State,
> To end her Picture, does the third time wait.[8]

Among various styles of representation that might be appropriate to the third year of the war, we are reminded of Pliny's story of how Protogenes, during his painting of Jalysus, had both relieved his frustration and achieved his desired effect with a luckily thrown sponge; that is to say, the replacement of art by accident:

> The Painter so, long having vext his cloth,
> Of his Hound's Mouth to feign the raging froth,
> His desperate Pencil at the work did dart,
> His Anger reacht that rage which past his Art;
> Chance finisht that which Art could but begin,
> And he sat smiling how his Dog did grinn.

(ll. 21–6)

Later Marvell alluded to the ancient painter Apelles, to the early modern Rubens, to the theme of monstrosity, to the mind–body distinction in the *paragone* between the sister arts; and he concluded with the hope that, suitably advised, Charles II would be able to renovate the tradition, and take over his own representation:

> Painter adieu, how well our Arts agree;
> Poetick Picture, Painted Poetry.
> But this great work is for our Monarch fit,
> And henceforth Charles only to Charles shall sit.
> His Master-Hand the Ancients shall out-do
> Himself the Poet and the Painter too.

(ll. 943–8)

The 'Last Instructions' has a more explicitly parliamentary focus than its predecessors (that is, it presents the debates in the House of Commons as to how the costs of the war are to be met as themselves a mock-heroic battle). But since it must now add to the previous débâcles the naval disaster that occurred in June 1667, when the Dutch fleet sailed up the Thames and the Medway and burned the English fleet as it lay at anchor at Chatham, it returns to the theme of bravery versus cowardice, and makes the remarkable suggestion that the only truly heroic figures in this third year of the war are the Scotsman Archibald Douglas, who burned to death on his ship, and the Dutch commander De Ruyter, both of whom are treated to loving and lavish idealization.

One of the oddest conclusions in the poem's immense catalogue of chicanery (though it was far from eccentric to Marvell's long-term concerns) is the passage in which he satirized the attempt to pass the buck for the Chatham disaster to a minor official of the dockyards, Peter Pett (another of Lely's Commonwealth subjects). On 31 October 1667, Marvell spoke in the Commons against sending Pett to the Tower. In September he had already written this absurdist passage into the 'Last Instructions':

> All our miscarriages on Pett must fall:
> His Name alone seems fit to answer all.
> Whose Counsel first did this mad War beget?
> .   .   .   .
> Who did advise no Navy out to set:
> And who the Forts left unrepair'd? Pett.
> .   .   .   .
> Who all our Ships expos'd in Chathams Net?
> Who should it be but the Phanatick Pett.

(ll. 767 ff.)

55

The suggestion clearly is that Pett is being made a scapegoat because of his Nonconformity.

This passage will serve to point us forward to Marvell's polemical tracts in defence of the Nonconformists against the more intemperate members of the Restoration church establishment. No reader of Marvell's poems should be ignorant of what he accomplished in *The Rehearsal Transpros'd*, of the mixture of jest and earnest by which he humiliated Samuel Parker, earned the wary hostility of John Dryden, and engaged the king himself as his behind-the-scenes patron and protector.

For the modern reader, early modern religious polemic is not a user-friendly genre. The issues are often obscured by the form known technically as 'animadversion', which required one tediously to answer an opponent by following the structure of his argument, even line by line. There was always the temptation, therefore, to focus on superficial mistakes or errors of taste in one's adversary's performance, which could make the animadverter seem little better than his prey. The issues, however, remain important even today, when religious fundamentalism has reappeared as a geopolitical concern. Roughly speaking, they divide into three categories: what it is proper to believe about things supernatural; what forms of worship are appropriate to the beliefs one holds; to what extent people should be compelled to adopt the majority belief of the country in which they happen to reside, and to what extent the secular power (the state) should engage itself in this compulsion.

The history of England in Marvell's lifetime was haunted by the afterlife of old struggles in all three of these categories. The Reformation as constituted by Henry VIII had made England willy-nilly a country that rejected papal authority and monasticism but maintained almost everything else that had accrued to Christianity as an institution. Protestantism as a reform movement in both doctrine and religious practice did not take hold, despite the brief Edwardian Reformation, until the second half of the sixteenth century, and even then Elizabeth's own religious conservativism ensured that there would be an active protest movement from the left – for want of a better term, puritanism – that would cry out unsuccessfully against the continued use of vestments and other formal reminders of Roman Catholic practice. This 'vestiarian' controversy soon merged with the question of church government:

although it had lopped off its papal head, was the Anglican church, with its vertical hierarchy of bishops and archbishops, anywhere sanctioned by scripture? When both Dryden and Samuel Parker accused Marvell of being the Martin Marprelate of the late seventeenth century, they recalled a series of scandalously funny pamphlets published under that pseudonym in the 1590s, attacking the bishops of the Elizabethan church for corruption, incompetence, and a brutal intolerance. Elizabeth managed, mostly by outright repression, to restrain her puritan subjects; but in the 1640s they returned in force, as the Presbyterians and other strongly Protestant subsets of the Long Parliament, who at last had matters under their own control. One more reversal brings us up to date with Marvell, whose own constituency letters, as we have seen, recorded the criminalization of the leaders of the 'Puritan revolution'; while the Act of Uniformity (1661) and the notorious Clarendon Code that followed it made lesser criminals of groups like the Quakers who preferred a simpler and more communal form of worship than that enjoined by the Restoration church.

It was an odd feature of this third phase of Anglican/Puritan controversy that the rhetorical stances formerly associated with each side changed hands. For it had been a strategy of Anglican debate to claim moderation, and to identify the would-be reformers as zealous extremists. In the 1660s, however, when the Nonconforming ministers were ejected from the pulpits, they themselves preached love, peace and patience under persecution. It is all the more startling, therefore, to read the preface to Samuel Parker's *Discourse of Ecclesiastical Politie* (1669). 'To lash these morose and churlish Zealots with smart and twingeing Satyrs is so farr from being a criminal Passion', wrote Parker, 'that 'tis a Zeal of Meekness and Charity ... nothing but Zeal can encounter Zeal'.[9]

There were others who responded to Parker, but they were not so rhetorically skilled as Marvell. Marvell, moreover, was emboldened to enter the dispute by the king's Declaration of Indulgence in 1672, which suspended all penal laws against both Roman Catholics and Nonconformists. Any suspicions Marvell may have had about the real intentions of the king's Declaration, which was unconstitutional and likely to benefit Roman Catholics considerably more than those at the other end of the confessional spectrum, could be left unspoken; for at the heart of his strategy was the claim that the king himself was in favour of religious toleration, and would therefore be horrified to learn what enforcements a member of his clergy was promoting. 'God be prais'd his Majesty is far of another temper' (p. 60). This strategy clearly resembled the final 'advices' to the king that concluded his satirical triptych.

Under this umbrella Marvell proceeded to characterize Parker (and by implication anyone who shared his views) as a false Crusader, a crazy Don Quixote, a mad dog, a persecuting Roman emperor like Nero or Caligula, and, by way of the allusion to the original *Rehearsal* written by the duke of Buckingham in mockery of John Dryden, as a braggadocio named Bayes, who was simultaneously the author of pretentious 'heroic' plays and their chief protagonist. Buckingham's play was first performed in December 1671, and appeared in print in 1672. Seeing his opportunity sharpened by Buckingham's attack on his old opponent, now poet laureate of the Restoration, Marvell brought all of his interests – politics, religion, and the use of literary talent therein – into effective correlation.

Among the hundreds of neat deflationary tricks that Marvell pulls on Parker, few can be as interesting to a modern reader as his reworking of that strange metaphor from his 'Dialogue between the Soul and Body' (an echo which again makes one wonder whether Marvell's devotional poems belong to the early 1650s). In his scathing mini-biography which opens the first part, Marvell remarked that Parker 'forgot not the main chance, but hearing of a vacancy with a Noble man, he clapp'd in, and easily obtained to be his Chaplain':

> This thing alone elevated him exceedingly in his own conceit, and raised his Hypocondria into the Region of the Brain: that his head swell'd like any Bladder with wind and vapour. But after he *was stretch'd to such an height in his own fancy, that he could not look down from top to toe but his Eyes dazled at the Precipice of his Stature*; there fell out, or in, another natural chance which push'd him headlong. (p. 30; italics added).

Puffed up by vanity and ambition, and misled by the admiration of the household servants, Parker became, in Marvell's metaphor, a parody of the Body that resists the idealizing impulses of the Soul.

It was not until the second part of *The Rehearsal Transpros'd*, however, that the structure of Marvell's intellectual challenge to Parker became fully visible. We should not overlook the letter he wrote to Sir Edward Harley before embarking on his sequel, in which he described being 'drawn in, I hope by a good Providence, to intermeddle in a noble and high argument' (*PL2*, pp. 328–9), implying that he took the charge very seriously indeed. The heart of Marvell's new profundity lies in his elaboration of one of the six 'Plays' to which he had reduced Parker's arguments, in this case the thesis of the 'Unlimited Magistrate'. In refuting the idea of a monarch with unlimited power over the religious life of his subjects, Marvell extended subtle warning to Charles (who had just been forced by parliament to withdraw the Declaration of Indulgence) against any further interference in ecclesiastical matters.

Marvell's strategy was to replace his opponent's all-or-nothing approach with a set of finer distinctions in which the sources, sanctions, and uses of power are carefully separated and analysed. This approach ties *The Rehearsal Transpros'd* to both the 'Horatian Ode' and 'The First Anniversary'. 'The Power of the Magistrate', he admits, 'does most certainly issue from the Divine Authority' (p. 232); but 'the *modester* Question' (a locution we should now recognize) is 'how far it is advisable for a Prince to exert and push the rigour of that Power which no man can deny him' (p. 233). And Marvell proceeded to emphasize not only the rightness, but also the prudential value of clemency and moderation, going so far as to suggest that a wise patience on the ruler's part will have the effect of depoliticizing his subjects, who will out of gratitude or carelessness cease to insist upon their constitutional rights. 'Dealing still in that fair and tender way of management, it is impossible but that even without reach or intention upon the Princes part, all should fall into his hand, and in so short a time the very memory or thoughts of any such thing as Publick liberty would, as it were by consent, expire and be for ever extinguish'd' (p. 234). The ironic cast to this recommendation is well concealed behind the circuitous syntax, which gives us 'impossible [that anything should happen] but that' instead of simply 'possible'. In place of that 'wondrous Order and Consent' that would arrive when Cromwell re-established constitutional government, Marvell now suggests that 'a great and durable design' to subvert the constitution might be completed, 'as it were by consent', by one of Charles's successors. Given his later *Account of the Growth of Popery and Arbitrary Government*, which labours to prevent any such disaster, we can be sure that Marvell believed nothing of the sort.

This serious argument, then, is what Marvell had in mind when he chose to define his stance as alternating (perhaps ricocheting would be a better description) 'betwixt Jest and Earnest' (p. 187) – an almost impossible balance to maintain. Modern readers will have to decide for themselves whether he did maintain it; but the success of his pamphlets at the time is undeniable. They set a new standard of wit in theological and political dispute that, though it built on the Martin Marprelate pamphlets, was infinitely more *literary* in its appeal to a network of intertextual relations, reputations and in-jokes. The classical satirists Horace and Juvenal, Donne's *Metempsychosis*, Hooker's *Laws of Ecclesiastical Polity*, Bacon's *Wise and Moderate Discourse*, Davenant's *Gondibert*, Hobbes's *Leviathan*, Montaigne's *Essays*, the *Cassandra* of Costes de la Calprenède, Sidney's *Arcadia*, Denham, Killigrew, Shakespeare's *Midsummer Night's Dream* and *The Merry Wives of Windsor*, Ogilby's *Fables*, Guarini's *Il Pastor Fido*, the Fathers of the Church, not to mention a vast array of historians, inhabit the pages of *The Rehearsal Transpros'd* and demand that we know who or what they are if Marvell's points are to find their target. This effortless display of scholarship and cultivation makes one realize what else Marvell had been doing alongside his parliamentary duties, and sets a standard of educational breadth that few professional politicians today are likely to exemplify.

Epilogue

Having reached the end of this brief introduction to Marvell, I must now partially repair my neglect of several marvellous poems, some of which are different enough from those discussed in the preceding chapters as to complicate Marvell's image still further. I would not, of course, want my redefinition of Marvell's achievements and preoccupations to divert readers away from the poems that are still most frequently anthologized, most likely to be taught, most fought over in rival interpretations, merely because I believe T. S. Eliot was mistaken in his estimate of what was 'really valuable' in Marvell's canon.

In fact, my delay in reaching these poems may have been beneficial, since all of the foregoing should help to explain, if never satisfactorily to define, the unique mixture of precision and mystery which has made certain poems so much the object of critical desire. The question of whether they are the most characteristic of his peculiar talents or, by other standards, slightly eccentric, off-duty, as it were, can now give place to the less tendentious question of whether we can understand them better in the context of his whole career. Take, for instance, the enigmatic sadomasochism of 'The Unfortunate Lover', with its mother 'split against the Stone, | In a Cesarian Section', and her bleeding son transformed into heraldry: 'In a Field Sable a Lover Gules'; the surrealism of the poem's account of the lover's heroic struggle with forces beyond his control is more intelligible as the imagination's response to the civil war than as a formal exercise in emblematics, not to mention a 'real' love poem (which would have to be homoerotic). The paradox of the Unfortunate Lover is that there is no *relationship* mentioned or even figured in the poem, and his solitariness as the centre of the storm, the eye of the hurricane, is what makes his suffering heroic. Who, then, speaks of him as 'my poor lover', the reader must inquire, and, deprived of any basis for a commonsense answer, begin to wonder about other kinds of meanings. Without exactly converting its extravagances into political allegory, the poem invites comparison with the emblematic broadsides that show the ship of state against a tempestuous background, lightning flashing down through black clouds, with the king as the discarded pilot being thrown overboard; and the 'Cesarian Section' which split the 'Mother' against the rock is more intelligible as an image of what happens to a country during civil war than of a human birth, however unusual.

Or consider the group of translucent poems grouped around the figure of the mower, Marvell's substitute for the less energetic shepherd of classical pastoral. While almost every ingredient of 'Damon the Mower' can be recognized as a brilliant comic reworking of Virgilian eclogue, the point of 'The Mower against Gardens' is considerably sharpened if we can see its relation both to Marvell's devotional poems (including 'Bermudas') and to his own self-ironization:

> Luxurious Man, to bring his Vice in use,
> Did after him the World seduce:
> And from the fields the Flow'rs and Plants allure,
> Where Nature was most plain and pure.
>
> .   .   .   .
>
> The Pink then grew as double as his Mind;
> The nutriment did change the kind.
>
> .   .   .   .
>
> Another World was search'd, through Oceans new,
> To find the Marvel of Peru.

In this anti-garden manifesto, Marvell is recognizable both as the double-minded aesthete, whose fallen nature denies Nature her pristine puritanism, and the exotic plant transplanted from the New World to enhance the garden-owner's status. Together with the passage from 'Upon Appleton House' that reproached Fairfax for cultivating his private gardens and neglecting his own country, 'The Garden of the World ere while', this poem provides a narrow bridge to and from the controlled sensuality of 'The Garden' and its transference of all worldly ambitions to an anerotic 'am'rous ... green'. The abstractions and imperatives lurking in these supposedly 'pastoral' poems can clearly be sensed without one's having been exposed to Marvell's value system elsewhere ('In such a Conjuncture, dear Will, what Probability is there of my doing any Thing to the Purpose?'); but perhaps such exposure makes the elegance of these poems seem more poignant, because we can guess how painfully it was earned during the days of tutoring or parliamentary committee work.

But the amorous green which replaces the conventional reds and whites of courtship in 'The Garden' scarcely prepares one for the peculiar frisson of 'The Nymph complaining for the death of her Faun', which reinstates the sexual allure of those colours with a vengeance (reminiscent of 'The Unfortunate Lover'):

> Upon the Roses it would feed,
> Until its Lips ev'n seem'd to bleed:
> And then to me would boldly trip,
> And print those Roses on my Lip.
>
> . . . .
>
> Had it liv'd long, it would have been
> Lillies without, Roses within.

(*PL*1, p. 26)

The nymph's transference of her own desire from 'unconstant Sylvio' to her pet fawn is linguistically in excess of the conventional minor genre (lament of a girl for her dead pet) to which this poem might otherwise be assigned. And it does not help the reader seeking to read more or less literally to hear echoes of the Song of Songs ('I am my beloved's and my beloved is mine. He feedeth among the lilies') and of the Redemption ('There is not such another in I The World, to offer for their sin') which suggest more than *her* confusion of registers, *her* incapacity to distinguish between levels of seriousness. Meanwhile, the poem is framed by historical time, in its first-line allusion to the 'wanton Troopers' who have casually shot the fawn in their destructive path across the country; like the 'Prelat's rage' of 'Bermudas', this small phrase introduces a specifically seventeenth-century drama. Whereas 'Bermudas' reminds us, however glancingly, of puritan escapees from such phases of repression as Laudian 'Thorough', 'The Nymph complaining' gives its speaker, if only for a moment, a view of the New Model Army appropriate to the daughter of a cavalier household.

When religion, sex and politics (the three forbidden topics of polite society) are swirled together in this way, it makes a heady brew. Encountering this poem in an anthology, out of the context of Marvell's other writings, leaves readers perhaps too free. In consequence, we have seen interpretations that turn 'The Nymph complaining' into a full-fledged religious allegory;[1] a study in female naïvety (the speaker is a very *little* girl, hence the childishness of some of her sentences and the bathos of some of her lines);[2] a feminist treatise about seduction, even rape and illegitimate birth;[3] an exercise in Derridean deconstruction.[4] This poem has made readers of this century so uncomfortable that they have moved to resolve their discomfort by exclusion and systematization. 'Something', wrote Rosalie Colie, 'is exhausted in this poem; but I am not quite sure what it is'.[5]

We know by now, however, that Marvell experimented in the territories between jest and earnest, negotiated between the soul and the body, held satire and idealism to be tools in the same project, and saw, without being fully able to explain, that religion, sex and politics are names for the different (and sometimes crossing) paths of desire towards its unknown object. If one can keep all of the conflicting ingredients in 'The Nymph complaining' alive and in tension with one another, the tension makes the poem work, and prevents it from collapsing into sentimentality. And the fourth path that desire takes – that for want of a better word we call 'art' but that sometimes requires to be understood as asceticism, not aestheticism – is actually a refusal to walk the other paths any more. When the nymph concludes her lament by imagining herself turned to a miraculous marble statue ('For ... I shall weep though I be Stone'), and the fawn cut out of a different and more precious material ('purest Alabaster'), we may be tempted to call her solution frigidity or escapism. But we might also see it as an almost pure expression of desire in its essence, from which the difference between the nymph's naïvety and Marvell's sophistication has been erased:

> For I would have thine Image be
> White as I can, though not as Thee.

This option will be available especially, I suggest, if we have followed Marvell in his hunting of Samuel Parker through the forest of *The Rehearsal Transpros'd*, and heard his final words: 'However I have spit out your dirty Shoon'.

And what of the poem which Eliot selected as the best example of Marvell's wit, the one in which that cultivated, gentlemanly voice Eliot valued 'speaks out uncommonly strong': that is, the wooing poem, 'To his Coy Mistress'? By beginning this study with the contradictions in the 'Nettleton' portrait of Marvell I have, it is to be hoped, left room in his profile for the icy and even sinister passion of that poem's central section, which transforms the classical *carpe diem* theme into an almost Freudian encounter of Eros with Thanatos:

> Thy Beauty shall no more be found;
> Nor, in thy marble Vault, shall sound
> My ecchoing Song: then Worms shall try
> That long preserv'd Virginity:
> And your quaint Honour turn to dust;
> And into ashes all my Lust.
> The Grave's a fine and private place,
> But none I think do there embrace.

(PL1, p. 28)

And yet, when new readers encounter this famous poem, they ought to be aware how very *few* of Marvell's poems (a bare six out of fifty, not counting the satires) could reasonably be defined as love poems in the conventional sense; that is to say, poems where the reader is expected to hear the speaking voice as *the* voice, the authentic feeling in charge of the poem, unmediated by some other perspective or frame.

Nor, I suggest, can we fully appreciate the memorable lines 'But at my back I alwaies hear I Times winged Charriot' unless we also know how Marvell himself defined memorability in the 'Horatian Ode'; how he came to value Cromwell's capacity to 'seize the day' and turn 'flowing Time', that endless river which closes above the heads of ordinary folk like ourselves leaving scarcely a ripple, into history and originality. ''Tis he the force of scatter'd Time contracts, I And in one Year the work of Ages act.' This is, I infer, how Marvell would have preferred to have been himself remembered – as a man whose sense of being a witness to momentous events allowed him to make intelligent use of his own relative insignificance. The Marvell of this study is, in short, very different from Eliot's. He is more like, but by no means identical with, Legouis's triangulated poet-puritan-patriot. The words I would use to describe him have been somewhat out of fashion, but perhaps they are due for recovery: a moderate, certainly, someone who could see the best and worst on most sides of the story, and who believed that moderation and mediation were always desirable and usually possible; a liberal, certainly, someone who cherished rather clear ideas (for the time) of constitutional government, freedom of speech and conscience; in religion, indecisive; in person, a sensualist, perhaps only of the language, perhaps also of the body; a good friend to Milton, who was infinitely more egocentric; someone who could be both a brave man and a coward, depending on the circumstances.

Notes

INTRODUCTION

1. For Sir Peter Lely's portraits of Cromwell and Pett, see Oliver Millar, *Sir Peter Lely 1618–80* (London, 1978), pp. 43, 47. For Lely's Commonwealth style, see C. H. Collins Baker, *Lely & the Stuart Portrait Painters*, 2 vols (London, 1912), vol. 1, p. 143, 160–2.
2. For the 'Nettleton' and 'Hollis' portraits, and their relation to the 1681 engraving, see Hilton Kelliher, *Andrew Marvell Poet & Politician 1621–1678* (London, 1978), pp. 80–2, 124. Another account of the portraits appears in John Dixon Hunt, *Andrew Marvell: His Life and Writings* (Ithaca, 1978), pp. 11–18. For my own view that Lely was the painter of the 'Nettleton' portrait, and that it derives from the early 1650s, see *Marvell and the Civic Crown* (Princeton, 1978), pp. 147–50. The attribution is supported by Marvell's own references to Lely and George Vertue's note of a portrait of Marvell by Lely in the possession of the Ashley family.
3. Here and subsequently, full documentation of these critical works is supplied in the Select Bibliography.
4. *Marvell and the Civic Crown* (Princeton, 1978), p. 4.
5. *Andrew Marvell: The Critical Heritage*, ed. Elizabeth Story Donno (London, 1978); hereafter cited as Donno.
6. *Poems and Letters*, ed. H. M. Margoliouth, rev. Pierre Legouis, 2 vols (Oxford, 1971), vol. 2, p. 166; italics added. Unless otherwise stated, all citations of Marvell's poetry are from this edition.
7. *The Rehearsal Transpros'd*, ed. D. I. B. Smith (Oxford, 1971), pp. 159–60.
8. But compare William Empson, 'The Marriage of Marvell', in *Using Biography* (Harvard, 1984), pp. 43–95.
9. See Bertrand Dobell, *PMLA*, 53 (1938), 367–92.
10. There had apparently been a plan, by Henry Herringman, to publish the elegy in *Three Poems to the happy memory of the most renowned Oliver, late Lord Protector of this Commonwealth*, by Mr. Marvell, Mr. Driden, Mr. Sprat. See *Stationers' Register*, 20 January 1659. But Herringman changed his mind, and the volume was published instead by William Wilson, with a poem by Edmund Waller in the place of Marvell's. See *Poems and Letters*, vol. 1, p. 332.
11. For more detail, see my 'Miscellaneous Marvell', in *The Political Identity of Andrew Marvell*, ed. Conal Condren and A. D. Cousins (Aldershot,

1990), pp. 188–212.

12. See *Marvell and the Civic Crown*, pp. 114–17. G. F. de Lord's arguments for Marvell's authorship of the 'Second' and 'Third Advice' were rejected by Warren Chernaik, 'Appendix: Manuscript evidence for the canon of Marvell's poems', in *The Poet's Time: Politics and Religion in the Work of Andrew Marvell* (Cambridge, 1983), 206–14, solely on the physical evidence of the Popple manuscript. He made no assessment of the poems themselves, and concluded that their authorship 'must still be considered uncertain' (p. 211). Subsequently, A. B. Chambers, in *Andrew Marvell and Edmund Waller* (University Park and London, 1991), pp. 111–32, situates himself somewhere in the middle, by calling the 'Second' and 'Third Advice' the 'Marvell' poems, and by declaring that 'it cannot be reasonable to approach the "Last Instructions" except by means of the prior poems since Marvell could not or at any rate did not leave them out of this own account' (p. 112).

13. As Warren Chernaik pointed out, *The Poet's Time: Politics and Religion in the Work of Andrew Marvell* (Cambridge, 1983), p. 207, supporting evidence for Marvell's *not* having written 'Thyrsis and Dorinda' has come to light. But the disinclination of English critics to take Popple as a serious witness may be seen in Margarita Stocker and Timothy Raylor, 'A New Marvell Manuscript: Cromwellian Patronage and Politics', *ELR* (1990), 106–61. This long article describes a version of 'Blake's Victory' discovered among the papers of Samuel Hartlib and addressed to 'His Highness', that is, Cromwell. Nowhere in the article, during which many inferences are drawn about Marvell's connections with Hartlib, is it observed that this text of the poem, in the hand of one of Hartlib's scribes, is *not* attributed to Marvell. Perhaps this would count as supporting evidence for his not having written it.

14. Lord, 'From Contemplation to Action: Marvell's Poetic Career', *Philological Quarterly*, 46 (1967), 207–24. This structure was adopted in Lord's edition, *Andrew Marvell: Complete Poetry* (New York, 1968).

15. Elizabeth Story Donno (ed.) *Marvell: The Complete Poems* (1972), pp. 11, 217–18.

CHAPTER 1. THE BIOGRAPHICAL RECORD

1. See J. Milton French, *Life Records of John Milton* (New Brunswick, 1954), vol. 3, pp. 322–34.

2. Hilton Kelliher, *Andrew Marvell Poet & Politician 1621–1678* (London, 1978), p. 32. This catalogue of the tercentenary exhibition of Marvell at the British Museum brought Marvell's biography up to date, including Kelliher's own discoveries.

3. Margoliouth retained the 1681 placement; Donno moved 'Bermudas' to

what she guessed was its chronological position between two topical or occasional poems, 'The Character of Holland' (perhaps mid 1653) and 'A Letter to Dr. Ingelo' (1653–4). But there is nothing in 'Bermudas' to *prevent* it having been written, say, in 1642, when Laud was executed, or, for that matter, in the 1670s, when the ferocity of prelates was again in evidence.

4. This mini-autobiography was designed to refute Samuel Parker's insinuation that the Marvells, father and son, had any political profile in 1650, which Marvell rejected as an 'errour in Chronology'.

5. See Milton, *The Readie & Easie Way to Establish a Free Commonwealth*, in *Complete Prose*, ed. D. M. Wolfe *et al.*, 8 vols (New Haven, 1953–82), vol. 7, pp. 340-404.

6. *Old Parliamentary History*, 23 (London, 1761) 54; *Journal of the House of Commons*, 8:209. Milton's nephew, Edward Phillips, also reported that Milton escaped punishment because of the intercession of certain members of parliament and the Privy Council. 'Particularly in the House of Commons, Mr. Andrew Marvell ... acted vigorously in his behalf.' See Helen Darbishire, *The Early Lives of Milton* (London, 1932), p. 74.

7. Compare his translation of John Friessendorff's pamphlet, mentioned above, and his earlier verse 'Letter to Dr. Ingelo, then with my Lord Whitlock, Ambassador from the Protector to the Queen of Sweden' (*PL1*, pp. 104–7).

8. In the diary of Sir Joseph Williamson (*Public Record Office*, SP 105/222, f. 127) is a note to the effect that a Mr. Carr reported that 'once came over a Parliament man under the name of Mr. George by du Moulin's order ... much like Mervell, but he could not say it was he'. Two other documents of June 1674 state that Marvell was going under the alias 'Mr. Thomas'.

9. See Anchitell Grey, *Debates of the House of Commons from the year 1667 to the year 1694* (London, 1769), vol. 1, pp. 70–1.

10.See D. I. B. Smith (ed.), *The Rehearsal Transpros'd*, p. xxii; citing *Historical Manuscripts Commission*, Report 7, p. 518A.

11.Smith (ed.) *The Rehearsal Transpros'd*, p. xx; citing Gilbert Burnet, *A Supplement to the History of My Own Time*, ed. H. C. Foxcroft, 3 vols (Oxford, 1897–1902), vol. 3, p. 216.

CHAPTER 2. RELIGION AND PLEASURE

1. Kitty Scoular Datta, 'New Light on Marvell's "A Dialogue between the Soul and Body"', *Renaissance Quarterly*, 22 (1969), 242–55; Rosalie Colie, *My Ecchoing Song': Andrew Marvell's Poetry of Criticism* (Princeton, 1970), pp. 115–17.

2. For a useful essay on the vogue for tear poems, in England probably generated by the Jesuit Robert Southwell's *'Marie Magdalens Funeral*

Teares', see Joan Hartwig, 'Tears as a Way of Seeing', in *On the Celebrated and Neglected Poems of Andrew Marvell*, eds. Claude Summers and Ted-Larry Pebworth (Columbia and London, 1992), pp. 70–85.

3. Compare, of course, 'To his Coy Mistress', and the 'coy Vision' of England who appears to Charles II in his bedroom at the end of the 'Last Instructions to a Painter'.

4. John Donne, *Poems*, ed. H. J. Grierson, 2 vols (Oxford, 1912), vol. 1, p. 318).

5. Among this poem's complexities is its relationship to 'Eyes and Tears', whose final stanza reintroduces the Magdalen (in Latin) as one who, having also abandoned her human loves (*lascivos quum dimisit Amantes*) restrains those same judgemental feet with a chain woven of penitence.

6. Marvell, *Complete Works*, ed. A. B. Grosart (repr. New York, 1966), vol. 4, pp. 177–8.

CHAPTER 3. HINDSIGHT AND FORESIGHT

1. The exception to this statement is that 'A Dialogue between Thyrsis and Dorinda' a curious pastoral poem about longing for death and immortality, intervenes between Marvell's poem on Admiral Blake's naval victory over a Spanish fleet in 1657 and 'The Character of Holland', which also celebrates the aggressive foreign policy of the Protectorate, with Cromwell featured as 'our Neptune' shaking a trident composed of 'those piercing Heads, Dean, Monck and Blake'.

2. See Cleanth Brooks, 'Criticism and History: Marvell's "Horatian Ode"', *Sewanee Review*, 55 (1947), 199–222; versus Douglas Bush, 'Marvell's "Horatian Ode"', *Sewanee Review*, 60, (1952), 362–76.

3. For the extensive bibliography that deals with Marvell's use of Roman texts in the 'Ode', the reader is referred to *Poems and Letters*, vol. 1, pp. 294–303. See also Blair Worden, 'Andrew Marvell, Oliver Cromwell and the Horatian Ode', in *Politics of Discourse*, eds. Kevin Sharpe and Steven Zwicker (Berkeley, Los Angeles and London, 1987), pp. 147–80.

4. See J. A. Mazzeo, 'Cromwell as Davidic King', in *Reason and the Imagination* (New York, 1962); John M. Wallace, 'Andrew Marvell and Cromwell's Kingship', *ELH*, 30 (1963), 209–35; *Destiny his Choice: The Loyalism of Andrew Marvell* (Cambridge, 1968), pp. 106–40. Contrast Stephen Zwicker, 'Models of Governance in Marvell's "The First Anniversary"', *Criticism*, 16 (1974), 1–12; A. M. Patterson, *Marvell and the Civic Crown*, pp. 68–90.

5. See Judges 8:22–3: 'Then the men of Israel said unto Gideon, Rule thou over us, both thou, and thy son, and thy son's son also: for thou hast delivered us from the hand of Midian. And Gidson said unto them, I will not rule over you, neither shall my son rule over you: the Lord shall rule over you.'

CHAPTER 4. JEST AND EARNEST

1. Cowley, *Poems* (London, 1656), p. 9.
2. See *Journal of the House of Commons*, 8:621.
3. See *Poems and Letters*, vol. 2, p. 47.
4. *Journal of the House of Commons*, 8:629, 654.
5. Dryden, *Works*, eds. E. N. Hooker and H. T. Swedenberg, Jr, (Berkeley and Los Angeles, 1961), vol. 1, pp. 50, 46.
6. I cite the 'Second' and 'Third Advice' from *Anthology of Poems on Affairs of State: Augustan Satirical Verse, 1660–1714*, ed. George de F. Lord (New Haven and London, 1975), pp. 31–59. The disadvantages of a modernized text are outweighed by the excellence of the annotation.
7. The reference is to Henry Bennet, earl of Arlington, married into the family of Nassau, and responsible for introducing Louise de Kéroualle to Charles II, who adopted her as his favourite mistress, along with her pro-French policies.
8. This intention was, however, subverted, first by the appearance of a 'Fourth' and 'Fifth' satirical advice, and by a fairly large number of other imitations. But none of the characteristics which are shared by the 'Second', 'Third' and 'Last' – that is, a consistent theoretical programme, an intelligent exploitation of details (and the same details) of the pictorialist tradition, and a thematization of the pictorial concept of advice so as to make it stand for political counsel also – appear in any of the other imitations.
9. Samuel Parker, *A Discourse of Ecclesiastical Politie, Wherein The Authority of the Civil Magistrate Over the Consciences of Subjects in Matters of External Religion is Asserted; The Mischiefs and Inconveniences of Toleration are Represented, And All Pretenses Pleaded in Behalf of Liberty of Conscience are Fully Answered* (London, 1669), pp. iii–ix.

EPILOGUE

1. Geoffrey Hartman, '"The Nymph Complaining ... " A Brief Allegory', *Essays in Criticism* (1968), pp. 113–35.
2. Rosalie Colie, *'My Ecchoing Song': Andrew Marvell's Poetry of Criticism* (Princeton, 1970), 88–90.
3. Jack E. Reese, 'Marvell's "Nymph" in a New Light', *Etudes Anglaises*, 18 (1965), 399–400.
4. Jonathan Goldberg, *Voice Terminal Echo: Postmodernism and English Renaissance Texts* (New York and London, 1986), 14–36.
5. Colie, *'My Ecchoing Song'*, p. 61.

Select Bibliography

BIBLIOGRAPHIES AND REFERENCE WORKS

André Marvell: poète, puritain, patriote, 1621–1678, by P. Legouis: Paris and London (1928). Contains a full, annotated bibliography, including a list of prose works attributed to Marvell.

Andrew Marvell, 1927–1967, by D. G. Donovan (London, 1969). One of the Elizabethan Bibliographies Supplements.

Andrew Marvell, A Reference Guide (Boston, 1981).

A Concordance to the English Poems of Andrew Marvell, by G. R. Guffey (Chapel Hill, 1974).

Recent Studies in Marvell, by Jerome Dees, in *English Literary Renaissance*, 22 (1992), 273–95.

Recent Studies in Marvell, by Gillian Szanto, in *English Literary Renaissance*, 5 (1975), 273–86.

EDITIONS OF WORKS BY MARVELL

Collections

Andrew Marvell, ed. F. Kermode and K. Walker (Oxford, 1990). Contains poetry (based on Margoliouth) and some prose, the partial text of *The Rehearsal Transpros'd* based on Smith (see below).

Complete Poems, ed. E. S. Donno (Harmondsworth, 1972). Penguin edition.

Complete Poetry, ed. G. de F. Lord (New York, 1968; repr. 1984). Reorganizes poetry in categories, and includes 'Second' and 'Third Advice'.

Latin Poetry, ed. W. A. McQueen and K. A. Rockwell (Chapel Hill, 1964).

Life and Lyrics, ed. M. Craze (1979). Prints forty of the best-known lyrics in assumed order of composition, with interspersed commentary.

Miscellaneous Poems (London, 1681). In all but two recorded copies the three 'Cromwell' poems have been cancelled. The British Library copy (C.59.i.8) contains the 'Horatian Ode', 'The First Anniversary', and ll. 1–184 of the 'Upon the Death of O.C.' A reprint of BL C.59.i.8 was published by the Nonesuch Press in 1923. A second reprint was published by the Scolar Press (Menston, 1969), with an Appendix reproducing corrections and additions to the 1681 edition made in

Bodleian MS Eng. poet. d. 49.

Poems, ed. H. Macdonald (London, 1952). Reprint of BL 1681 edition with some additional poems. Muses' Library edition.

Poems and Letters, ed. H. M. Margoliouth, 2 vols (Oxford, 1927, 1952; rev. P. Legouis, 1971). The definitive edition; the 1971 edition contains eight new letters and updated commentary on the poems.

Poems and Satires, ed. E. Wright (1904).

Selected Poetry, ed. F. Kermode (New York, 1967).

Selected Poetry and Prose, ed. D. Davison (London, 1952). Contains most of the poetry and a little prose.

Selected Poetry and Prose, ed. R. Wilcher (1986). Part of a series which aims to present texts in 'historical and critical context'.

Works, ed. T. Cooke, 2 vols (London, 1776). Contains the 1681 poems, State Poems, a short life of Marvell and a few letters. Reissued in 1772.

Works, ed. A. B. Grosart, 4 vols (Blackburn, 1872–5; repr. 1966). The first two volumes (1–*Poems*; 2–*Letters*) have been superseded by Margoliouth, but vols 3 and 4 remain the only collected edition of Marvell's prose works.

Works, ed. E. Thompson, 3 vols (London, 1776). Contains all the letters and poems of Cooke's edition, some new poems and satires, a life, and the bulk of the *Corporation Letters* and a few private ones.

Separate works

An Account of the Growth of Popery and Arbitrary Government. Appeared anonymously. A facsimile edition was published by the Heppenheim Press in 1971, intr. G. Salgado (Farnborough, 1971).

Mr. Smirke: Or, The Divine in Mode ... with A Short Historical Essay, concerning General Councils (London, 1676). Appeared anonymously. The *Essay* was reprinted alone in 1680 and 1687.

The Rehearsal Transpros'd (1672). Appeared anonymously with fictional imprint.

The Rehearsal Transpros'd: The Second Part (1673). Facsimile editions of both parts were published by Gregg International publishers in 1971.

The Rehearsal Transpros'd and the Rehearsal Transpros'd, The Second Part, ed. D. I. B. Smith (Oxford, 1971). The definitive edition of these tracts.

Remarks upon a Late Disingenuous Discourse (London, 1678). Appeared anonymously.

CRITICAL AND BIOGRAPHICAL STUDIES

Allen, D. C., *Image and Meaning: Metaphoric Traditions in Renaissance Poetry* (Baltimore, 1960; rev. 1968). Erudite study of traditional images and symbols; important essay on 'Upon Appleton House'.

Berger, H., *Second World and Green World: Studies in Renaissance Fiction Making* (Berkeley, Los Angeles and London, 1988), pp. 251–323. Blends three previously published essays, on the 'Nymph Complaining', 'The Garden', and 'Upon Appleton House', under the theme of withdrawal and return.

Brooks, C., 'Criticism and Literary History: Marvell's "Horatian Ode"', *Sewanee Review*, 55 (1947), 199–222.

Bush, D., 'Marvell's "Horatian Ode"', *Sewanee Review*, 60 (1952), 362–76. Together these two essays constitute the classic dispute between New Criticism and 'old' Historicism.

Chambers, A. B., *Andrew Marvell and Edmund Waller: Seventeenth Century Praise and Restoration Satire* (University Park and London, 1991). An enlightening comparison/relationship study.

Chernaik, W. L., *The Poet's Time: Politics and Religion in the Work of Andrew Marvell* (Cambridge, 1983). Analyses the 'Cromwell' and 'Fairfax' poems, the satires and polemical prose as a 'delicate equilibrium between historical necessity and individual choice'.

Colie, R. L., *'My Ecchoing Song': Andrew Marvell's Poetry of Criticism* (Princeton, 1970). Subtle and learned approach to Marvell as sophisticated experimenter with conventions and genres.

Condren, C., and A. D. Cousins (eds.), *The Political Identity of Andrew Marvell* (Aldershot, 1990). Contains a fine essay by N. H. Keeble on Marvell's constituency letters.

Cullen, P., *Spenser, Marvell and Renaissance Pastoral* (Cambridge, Mass., 1970).

Dixon Hunt, J., *Andrew Marvell: His Life and Writings* (London, 1978).

Eliot, T. S., 'Andrew Marvell', first printed in the *Times Literary Supplement*, 31 March 1921, pp. 201–3; repr. in *Andrew Marvell, 1621–78: Tercentenary Tributes* (London, 1922). The founding essay for Marvell's modernist reputation.

Empson, W., *Seven Types of Ambiguity* (London, 1930).

— — *Some Versions of Pastoral* (London, 1935; repr. 1966). Both volumes contain brilliant readings of Marvell's poems that render them classics of criticism.

Everett, Barbara, 'The Shooting of the Bears: Poetry and Politics in Andrew Marvell', in *Andrew Marvell: Essays on the tercentenary of his death*, ed. R. L. Brett (Oxford, 1979) pp. 62–103. A scattered but consistently intelligent attempt to deal both with the entire career and with Marvell's history of reception in this century.

Farley-Hills, D., *The Benevolence of Laughter: Comic Poetry of the Commonwealth and Restoration* (London and Basingstoke, 1974). Contains a chapter on 'Last Instructions'.

Friedman, D. M., *Marvell's Pastoral Art* (London, 1970). Argues that pastoral is Marvell's characteristic 'way of literary thinking'.

Haley, K. H. D., *William of Orange and the English Opposition, 1672–74* (1953).

Discusses the evidence that Marvell was a secret agent for the pro-Dutch party.

Kelliher, H., *Andrew Marvell: Poet and Politician, 1621–78*. (London, 1978). Catalogue for the British Library Exhibition celebrating the tercentenary; important biographical information.

Klause. J., *The Unfortunate Fall, Theodicy and the Moral Imagination of Andrew Marvell* (Hamden, Conn. 1983). A refreshingly idiosyncratic account of Marvell's career, with a stress on religious and philosophical problems.

Legouis, P., *André Marvell: poète, puritain, patriote, 1621–78* (Paris and London, 1928). The most complete critical biography, not yet superseded.

— — *Andrew Marvell, Poet, Puritan, Patriot, 1621–78* (Oxford, 1965). An abridged English version of the above, with updated references to subsequent scholarship.

Leishman, J. B., *The Art of Marvell's Poetry* (London, 1966). Interested in fine stylistic distinctions and comparisons with other poets.

Lord, G. de F., 'Two New Poems by Marvell', in *Evidence for Authorship: Essays on Problems of Attribution*, eds. D. V. Erdman and E. G. Fogel (Ithaca, 1966).

— — 'From Contemplation to Action: Marvell's Poetical Career', *Philological Quarterly*, 46 (1967), 207–24.

Nevo, R., *The Dial of Virtue: A Study of Poems on Affairs of State in the Seventeenth Century* (Princeton, 1963).

Patterson, A. M., *Marvell and the Civic Crown* (Princeton, 1978). An earlier, more detailed version of the present study, with a focus on rhetorical strategies.

Patrides, C. A. (ed.), *Approaches to Marvell: the York Tercentenary Lectures* (London, 1978). Contains a fine essay by B. K. Lewalski on the religious poems, and an appealingly puzzled attempt by J. Carey to define the 'constricted' quality of Marvell's imagination.

Rivers, I., *The Poetry of Conservatism 1600–1745: A Study of Poets and Public Affairs from Jonson to Pope* (Cambridge, 1973), pp. 101–25. A deft and judicious summary of Marvell's career.

Stocker, M., *Apocalyptic Marvell: The Second Coming in Seventeenth Century Poetry* (Athens, Ohio, 1986). Attempts to restore coherence to our fragmented Marvell by showing his long-term commitment to apocalyptic belief.

Toliver, H. E., *Marvell's Ironic Vision* (New Haven, 1965). Explaining irony as deriving from Platonic anti-worldliness, this study focuses only on the poems.

Wallace, J. M., *Destiny his Choice: The Loyalism of Andrew Marvell* (Cambridge, 1968). Deals primarily with the 'Cromwell' poems, satires and prose, in order to identify Marvell's political stance; a final chapter on 'Upon Appleton House'.

Wilcher, R., *Andrew Marvell* (Cambridge, 1985). An introduction to the

Marvell canon, with a bibliography.

Worden, B., 'Andrew Marvell, Oliver Cromwell, and the Horatian Ode', in *Politics of Discourse: The Literature and History of Seventeenth-Century England*, eds. K. Sharpe and S. N. Zwicker, pp. 147–80. Perhaps the best of many fine essays on the 'Ode'.

Index

Abimelech, 42
Albermarle, General George Monck,
    duke of, 17, 51, 54
Anglicans, 36, 57
Anglo-Dutch wars, 50-5
Annesley, Arthur, 21
Apelles, 49, 54
Arlington, Henry Bennet, earl of, 19,
    52
Arundel, 49

Bacon, Sir Francis, 60
    Wise and Moderate Discourse, 60
Blake, Admiral Robert, 9, 31
Boulter, Robert, 7, 8
Bradshaw, John, 12
Browne, Sir Thomas, 6
Buckingham, George Villiers, first
    duke of, 49
    Rehearsal, 58
Burnet, Bishop Gilbert, 21

Caesar, Augustus, 37
Caesar, Julius, 37, 40
Calprenède, Costes de la, 60
    Cassandra, 60
Cambridge, 12, 22, 23, 29
Carew, Thomas, 4
Carlisle, Charles Howard, earl of, 18
Carr, Robert, viscount Rochester, earl
    of Somerset, 49
cavaliers, 8, 13, 63
censorship, 7
Charles I, 4, 9, 34, 35, 37, 38, 39, 42,
    49, 50
Charles II, 8, 13, 15, 17, 18, 19, 20,
    50, 53, 55, 59
    Declaration of Indulgence, 20, 57,
    59
Clarendon, *see* Hyde
Clarke, George, 9
Cleveland, John, 4
Coke, Sir Edward, 43
Colie, Rosalie, 4, 25, 64

Cooke, Thomas Hesiod, 3, 22
Counter-Reformation, 25, 29
Cowley, Abraham, 4, 49
Crashaw, Richard, 4, 6, 26
    'The Weeper', 26
Croft, Bishop Herbert, 36
    Naked Truth, 36
Cromwell, Oliver, 13-16, 18, 28, 51,
    59, 65
    death of, 15, 16
    poems about, 7-9, 11, 13-15, 31,
    34-45
    portrait of, 2
Cromwell, Richard,16, 17, 18, 37, 45

Danson, Thomas, 6
    De Causa Dei, 6
Datta, Kitty Scoular, 25
Davenant, Sir Willam, 60
    Gondibert, 60
Denham, Sir John, 9, 60
Donne, John, 4, 6, 32
    'La Corona', 32
    Metempsychosis, 60
Donno, Elizabeth Story, 3, 4, 10, 26
Douglas, Archibald, 55
Downing, George, 16
Dryden, John, 18, 51, 56, 57, 58
    Annus Mirabilis, 18, 51
Dutton, William, 13, 23
Dyke, Anthony Van, 49, 50

Eikon Basilike, 35
Eliot, T. S., 3-5, 11, 34, 61, 64, 65
Elizabeth I, 56, 57
Exclusion Crisis, 7

Fairfax, Mary, 12, 47
Fairfax, Sir Thomas, 8, 9, 11, 12, 13,
    29-30, 34-5, 45-7, 62
Fifth Monarchists, 14
Finch, Sir Heneage, 18
Fire of London, 51
Four Days' Battle, 51

Friedman, Donald, 4
Gibson, Richard, 53, 54
Gideon, 40, 42
Greek Anthology, 51
Grierson, H. J., 4
Grosart, Alexander, 11
   Complete Works, 11
Guarini, Giovanni Battista, 60
   Il Pastor Fido, 60

Harley, Sir Edward, 58
Hawkins, Henry, 25
   Parthenia Sacra, 25
Hayes, James, 19
Henry VIII, 29, 56
Herbert, George, 6, 32
   'A Wreath', 32
Herrick, Robert, 6
Hobbes, Thomas, 43, 60
   Leviathan, 60
Holland, 18, 50-5
Hollis, Thomas, 2
Hooker, Richard, 60
   Laws of Ecclesiastical Polity, 60
Horace, 37, 53, 60
   Ars Poetica, 49
   'Cleopatra Ode', 37
Howe, John, 6, 32
Hugo, Hermann, 25, 28
   Pia Desideria, 25
Hull, 5, 12, 15, 17, 18, 21, 50
Hyde, Edward, earl of Clarendon, 53

James I, 49
James, duke of York, *see* York
Jesuits, 22, 25, 28
Jolt on Michaelmas Day, A
   (anonymous), 41
Jonson, Ben, 6
Jotham, 42, 47
Juvenal, 60

Kelliher, Hilton, 12, 13, 15, 22
Killigrew, Thomas, 60

L'Estrange, Sir Robert, 19, 21
Laud, Archbishop, William, 13
Legouis, Pierre, 2, 9, 10, 11, 65
Leishman, J. B., 4
Lely, Sir Peter, 1, 2, 49, 53, 55
Levellers, 43, 47
Lord, George de F., 9, 10, 26
Lovelace, Richard, 6, 13

Lowestoft, battle of, 50
Lucan, 37
   Pharsalia, 37
Luttrell, Narcissus, 8

Machiavelli, Niccolò, 13
Margoliouth, H. M., 10, 34
Marprelate, Martin, 20, 57, 60
Marvell, Andrew:
   *Account of the Growth of Popery
     and Arbitrary Government*, 6,
     11, 59
   'Bermudas', 13, 22, 30-2, 62, 63
   biography, 5-6, 7, 12-13, 15-21,
     22-3, 25, 28-30, 34-5, 46-7, 50,
     52, 55, 65-6
   'The Character of Holland', 50
   'The Coronet', 32
   Cromwell and, 7-9, 13-16, 18, 28,
     31, 34-47, 51, 59, 65
   'Damon the Mower', 62
   'Dialogue between a Resolved
     Soul, and Created Pleasure',
     22
   'Dialogue between the Soul and
     Body', 25, 29, 30, 58
   'Elegy upon the Death of My
     Lord Francis Villiers', 9
   'Epigramma in Duos Montes', 46
   'Eyes and Tears', 25-6
   'The First Anniversary of the
     Government Under His
     Highness the Lord Protector',
     7, 14, 15, 31, 38, 39-45, 47, 59
   'The Garden', 1, 31, 62, 63
   Historical Essay [on] General
     Councils, 5
   'An Horatian Ode on Cromwel's
     Return', 7, 13, 34-40, 44-5, 59,
     65
   'Justice of the Swedish Cause',
     15
   'Last Instructions to a Painter', 2,
     8, 10, 18, 49, 54, 55
   Mercurius Politicus, 14
   Milton and, 3, 4, 5, 12, 14, 15, 17,
     24, 28, 44
   *Mr. Smirke: Or, the Divine in
     Mode*, 5, 20
   Miscellaneous Poems, 2, 7-10, 12,
     22, 34
   'The Mower Against Gardens', 62

Nonconformity and, 18-21, 24, 30-1, 36, 51, 54, 56, 57
'Nymph complaining for the death of her Faun', 11, 63, 64
'On a Drop of Dew', 22, 26-8, 30
'On the Victory Obtained by Blake over the Spaniards', 9, 31
Parker, Samuel and, 20-1, 24, 48, 56-9, 64
in parliament, 6, 12, 15, 16-20, 44-5, 51-2, 55, 60
'Poem Upon the Death of His Late Highness the Lord Protector', 7, 34
Poems on Affairs of State, 8
'Popple MS', 9-10, 49
portraits of:
　'Hollis portrait', 1
　'Nettleton portrait', 1, 2, 64
pseudonyms of:
　'Churche's jester', 20, 21
　'the Relator', 21
　Rivetus, Andreas, 36
The Rehearsal Transpros'd, 5, 11, 16, 20, 23, 48, 56, 58, 59, 60, 64
The Rehearsal Transpros'd: The Second Part, 5, 16, 23, 48, 58
religious toleration and, 11, 36, 57-60
Remarks upon a Late Disingenuous Discourse, 6, 32
Roman Catholicism and, 23-30, 56-7
'Second Advice to a Painter', 9, 10, 49, 51, 52, 53
'Third Advice to a Painter', 9, 10, 18, 49, 53
'Thyrsis and Dorinda', 9
'To His Coy Mistress', 11, 64, 65
'Tom May's Death', 9
'The Unfortunate Lover', 61-3
'Upon the Hill and Grove in Bill-borow', 46
'Upon Appleton House', 20, 30, 46, 62
Marvell, Andrew Sr, 12, 22
Matthias, Mr., 9
May, Thomas, 37
Michelangelo, Buonarotti, 49, 51, 54
Milton, John, 3, 4, 5, 12, 14, 15, 17, 24, 28, 44

Monck, Anne, duchess of George Monck, duke of Albermarle, 54
Monck, General, *see* Albermarle
Montaigne, Michel de, 60

New Criticism, 4, 34, 40
Newcomb, Thomas, 7
Noah, 40, 52, 53
Nonconformists, 13, 18, 19, 20, 21, 24, 30-1, 36, 51, 54, 56, 57

Ogilby, John, 60
　Fables, 60
Oxenbridge, John, 13, 23

Parker, Samuel, 20, 21, 24, 48, 56, 57, 58, 59, 64
　Discourse of Ecclesiastical Politie, 57
Parliament, 4, 6, 7, 8, 12, 13, 15, 16-19, 44-5, 50-2, 55, 57, 60
　Act of Uniformity, 18, 57
　Clarendon Code, 57
　Conventicle Act, 19, 20
　House of Commons, 8, 15, 18, 19, 50, 52, 55
　House of Lords, 17, 18
　Long Parliament, 57
Pett, Peter, 2, 55, 56
Philips, Katherine, 6
Pliny, 37, 49, 54
Ponder, Nathaniel, 21
Pope, Alexander, 28
　'Eloisa to Abelard', 28
Popple, William, 3, 6, 9, 19
Protectorate, 8, 40, 42, 44
Protogenes, 49, 54

Quakers, 57

Rivers, Isabel, 5
Rubens, Peter Paul, 49, 54
Rupert, Prince, 51
Ruyter, Admiral Michael de, 55

Sanderson, Sir William, 50
　Graphice, 50
Scott, Thomas, 17
Scudamore, James, 13
Shakespeare, William, 26, 60
　Comedy of Errors, 26
　Merry Wives of Windsor, 60
　Midsummer Night's Dream, 60
Sidney, Sir Philip, 60

Arcadia, 60
Smith, D. I. B., 11
Spelman, Sir Henry, 42

Tate, Nahum, 3
Thomason, George, 14
Thompson, Edward, 8, 9
Thurloe, John, 15, 16, 17
Thwaites, Isabella, 29
Toland, John, 3
Trott, Sir John, 7, 10

Vane, Sir Henry, 42
Villiers, Lord F., 9, 10

Wallace, John M., 42
Waller, Edmund, 49, 51, 53
    *Instructions to a Painter, For the
    Drawing of the Posture and
    Progress of His Majesties Forces
    at Sea*, 51
Wither, George, 41
    Vaticinium Causuale, 41
Wood, Anthony à, 8
Wordsworth, William, 3

York, James, duke of, 8, 50

Zeuxis of Croton, 49, 50